D0105430

VALDOSTA CHURCH OF CHRIST
Tuscumbia, Alabama

Staying Power

Staying Power

How You Can Win in Life's Tough Situations

Anne & Ray Ortlund

OLIVER NELSON

A Division of Thomas Nelson Publishers

Nashville • Atlanta • Camden • New York

Copyright © 1986 by Anne and Ray Ortlund

All rights reserved. Written permission must be secured from the publisher to use or reproduce any part of this book, except for brief quotations in critical reviews or articles.

Published in Nashville, Tennessee, by Oliver-Nelson Books, a division of Thomas Nelson, Inc., Publishers, and distributed in Canada by Lawson Falle, Ltd., Cambridge, Ontario.

Unless otherwise noted, the Bible version used in this publication is The Holy Bible: New International Version. Copyright © 1973, 1978, 1984, International Bible Society. Used by permission of Zondervan Bible Publishers.

Scripture quotations noted NKJV are from the NEW KING JAMES VERSION. Copyright © 1979, 1980, 1982, Thomas Nelson, Inc., Publishers.

Scripture quotations noted KJV are from the King James Version

Verses marked TLB are taken from *The Living Bible,* copyright 1971 by Tyndale House Publishers, Wheaton, IL. Used by permission.

Printed in the United States of America.

Library of Congress Cataloging-in-Publication Data

Ortlund, Anne.
Staying power.

1. Christian life—1960- . 2. Success.
I. Ortlund, Raymond C. II. Title.
BV4501.2.07273 1986 248.4 86-5192
ISBN 0-8407-9055-4

D E D I C A T I O N

There are six people in our lives who have "hung in there" with us through thick and thin in the ministry God has given us in these recent years. They are the three couples who comprise the Board of Directors of Renewal Ministries, and to them we lovingly dedicate this book:

Bruce and Adaline Bare
Jim and Peggy Dickson
Dick and Betty Thomas

CONTENTS

P R E F A C E

They say that inside every fat book is a thin book struggling to get out. As we wrote this one, our hearts were so full that it was difficult not to make the book too full as well!

The need for a call to perseverance, to staying power, is tremendous. Everywhere these days Christians are tempted to give up and drop out. Plenty of them are even doing it—greatly damaging both themselves and the whole body of Christ.

And so this book. Thanks to our dear Melinda DeVito for word processing the manuscript.

Lord, use this book! Use it to help Your children worldwide to become "established, strengthened, settled."

Ray and Anne Ortlund
Newport Beach, California
August 26, 1985

CHAPTER 1

Calm Down, Toughen Up!

How do you explain the people who "calm down and toughen up" through tears and toil and trial until they finally make it?

How do you explain Glenn Cunningham, who was burned so severely in a school fire that doctors said he'd never walk again—but who in 1934 set a world's record by running a mile in 4 minutes and 6.8 seconds?

How do you explain Itzhak Perlman, born of parents who survived a Nazi concentration camp, and himself paralyzed from the waist down when he was four years old, who became one of the world's truly great concert violinists?

How do you explain a little fellow who was called a slow learner, even retarded, but who grew up to be Albert Einstein?

And how do you explain the unknowns, the little people you and we would like to relate to, who also go through hard situations and come out winners?

We know a pastor named Steve whose congregation gave him nothing but trouble for seven long years. Eventually this so discouraged his wife, Jane, that she escaped into alcoholism, drugs, and unfaithfulness.

But Steve just wouldn't quit. Through grit, through tears, he just kept on loving his congregation and loving his wife.

There finally came a point when Jane was willing to go for help, and their relationship, through a long, slow, tedious, and sometimes painful process, is getting beautifully healed. Steve and Jane are at last truly in love.

Meanwhile, several of his most "ornery" church members moved away, and some really supportive ones moved in! Gradually the majority of the congregation began to lean toward the new leadership, and the climate of the church as a whole has slowly shifted from hostility to allegiance.

It all took time. It's not perfect yet, but it's good, and Steve's a happy man.

"But," you may be saying, "how do you know if I stick out my situation I'd get a happy ending like these you've talked about? Maybe I wouldn't. And this is the only life I've got."

Maybe.

We don't want to lead you into unrealistic dreaming, but . . . hear another story.

We have a friend Julia; she's in her late sixties. Long ago when Julia was in her twenties, her husband had a stroke which left him permanently paralyzed and speechless.

It could have easily buckled her knees, but it didn't. For almost a quarter of a century—until he died—Julia faithfully cared for her husband. She raised her young family alone. She took an active part in community and church life. Julia just did what she knew she could do, and she kept going.

After the death of her husband, everyone was thrilled when Julia fell in love with a very eligible bachelor her age from a nearby church. Eventually they were engaged.

The very week of the wedding—unexplainably—the fellow took his life.

The grief was intense; the pain was terrible; but Julia

just kept going. She gave herself to others; she never missed a beat in her civic and church responsibilities. She went through the right motions; she survived.

Today Julia is married to a silver-haired, vigorous, handsome fellow who fits her lifestyle well. He loves to share with her the larger leadership responsibilities she's so good at. Julia is truly fulfilled, and all of us who have witnessed her life are cheering her on.

Well, on a scale of one to ten, how is life for you right now?

Is it a one—and you wish you could start running and never look back?

Is it a five—and you're feeling discontented and you'd like to switch to something fresh?

Is it an eight—it's pretty good, but there are one or two bad parts you'd like to get rid of?

Maybe your first need is for techniques of staying power. Maybe you need to learn how to tackle the bad situations where you are and turn them around for good.

The two of us are no heroes, like Glenn Cunningham or Itzhak Perlman, but we've had troubles, too. There have been periods when we've cried to the Lord that our marriage was a mistake. And there have been times when one or both of us—rightly or wrongly—have felt unneeded, unloved, rejected by the other.

But all in all, our forty years together have been wonderful, especially the last five! We're just crazy about each other now, and more in love than ever before.

Or take our career in Christian ministry. We've had thirty-six years so far, and sometimes we wouldn't have given you a nickel for the whole bloomin' business. There was a time when the entire governing board of our church was against our remaining as pastor, and another time when a few people got long lists of signatures petitioning our removal. You better believe it, those were times of bewilderment and depression.

Yet over the long haul we've seen, and we're still seeing, the realization of fabulous dreams, and we wouldn't trade careers with anybody in the world.

But plenty are quitting . . . around you and around us.

These are restless, unstable days, and everywhere jobs are quit too soon, schooling is cut too soon, marriages are severed too soon, friendships are broken too soon—switching and dropping out have become epidemic.

The two of us feel it's time to cry, "Hold it! Wait! Reconsider! You don't have to quit! There are techniques available for hanging on and letting God turn bad situations into good!"

Listen:

The best way out is usually through.

In a throwaway society, consider holding on.

It's time to learn ways to "calm down and toughen up"! It's time to develop staying power—so that in life's tough situations, you can win.

The most
meaningless statistic
in a ball game
is the score
at halftime

CHAPTER 2

All Your Projects Have Three Time Periods

What's the secret that will build into you tenacity—through the toughest periods of your life—and make you come out on the other side a winner?

There's the story about a very fat office worker who decided to go on a diet. One of his new resolutions was to take a different route to work so he wouldn't pass his favorite bakery.

So everybody was surprised when the fat fellow shuffled into work one day carrying a huge coffee cake just oozing with frosting and goodies.

"This is different; this is special," he explained. "By mistake I went by the bakery this morning, and this was right in the window looking at me. So I said, 'Lord, if You want me to buy that, let there be a parking space right in front of the bakery.'

"And, sure enough, the eighth time around, there it was!"[1]

What's the secret that could have helped this fellow say no to coffee cakes and yes to a better weight?

We heard about another fellow running the Boston Marathon, who passed a tavern called "The Happy Swallow" that always offered free beers to the runners.

1. Jim Grant (Wimberly, Tex.). Quoted in "Life in These United States," *Reader's Digest,* April 1984, p. 78.

He dashed in, downed a beer, disappeared down the block, turned around, dashed back, and spent the rest of the afternoon at "The Happy Swallow."[2]

You may not identify with choosing between a bar and a marathon (we don't, either), but you, too, may feel somewhere along the way that you need a boost getting through your crunch periods—

Through hard times in your marriage,
In your job,
In your schooling,
In a relationship,
In your finances. . . .

Is there a secret that could help you stick it out through your darkest, most trying situations, until you emerge truly victorious? How do you get the staying power?

When you think about it, everybody's had those periods. And *the people who have made it have come through a time sequence—a time sequence that could be the clue to your making it, too:*

A. *They began,* in some new situation or effort;
B. *They hit problems and somehow worked their way through them;*
C. *They came out on top.*

For instance, the two of us are writing this book.

A. *We began* (with ideas, discussions, filled notebook pages, and memos on scraps of paper).
B. Now *we're persevering* (with scraps of paper all over our writing area, other "to do's" postponed, *more*

2. Mark Bricklin in "Prevention," *Reader's Digest,* April 1984, p. 144.

scraps of paper, writing and rewriting, more scraps of paper, more discussions, losing valuable scraps of paper, now's the time not to quit, typing, hassle, we're off the subject, cut that, scraps of paper, word processing, blizzards of scraps of paper, a manuscript begins to emerge, cut half of it, too long, too dull, it's terrible, where's that important scrap of paper, keep going . . .).

C. Eventually, God helping us, *we'll win!* Think about that pattern in the Bible. Over and over . . .

A. *God would begin*—with a person or a group.

B. *He'd take them through a process,* through pain and hassle, for testing and for toughening—

C. And *He'd bring them through triumphantly.*

The pattern seems to be: *begin, persevere, win!* For instance, there was Noah:

A. Noah walked with God.

B. Then came the threat of an impending flood. But Noah trusted God and obeyed Him . . .

C. And Noah emerged with his family intact, to start life again.

You see the pattern: *begin, persevere, win!* Or look at the whole nation of Israel:

A. God promised them the land of Canaan.

B. In a few generations they were in a completely different country, in deep trouble. But they trusted and obeyed. . . .

C. And eventually into the land of Canaan they went. *Begin—persevere—win!*

How about the sailors in Psalm 107:23–30? Or Joseph? Or David? Or young Daniel? God brought each of them through the same A-B-C process.

Whatever part of your life you're thinking about—school, marriage, job, relationship—

> Every undertaking of your life incorporates three periods of time. Recognize when you're in each one, follow certain principles prescribed for each, and He'll bring you through.
>
> *Begin, persevere, win! A, B, C!*

The A Zone is the initial stage of anything. It's the first week of school or of work; it's the honeymoon; it's the delight of a new friendship. We could say it looks like this:

A ZONE

Desire to ACHIEVE

Characterized by idealism, perhaps naivete, and maybe also apprehension. Attitude toward the future: hope for success

The B Zone has arrived when problems begin to crop up:

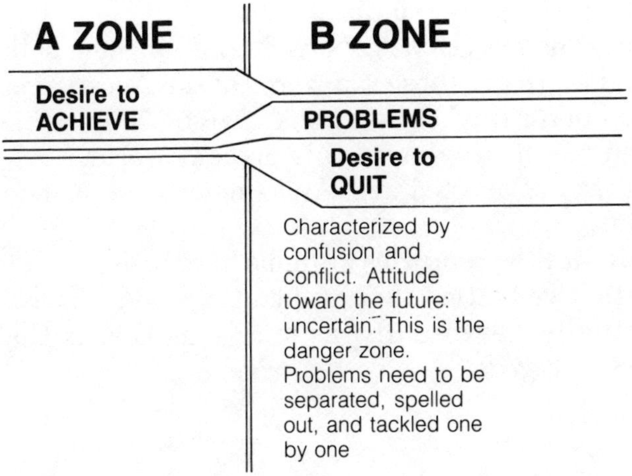

The B Zone will end in one of two ways. Maybe you will quit, and the project will abort:

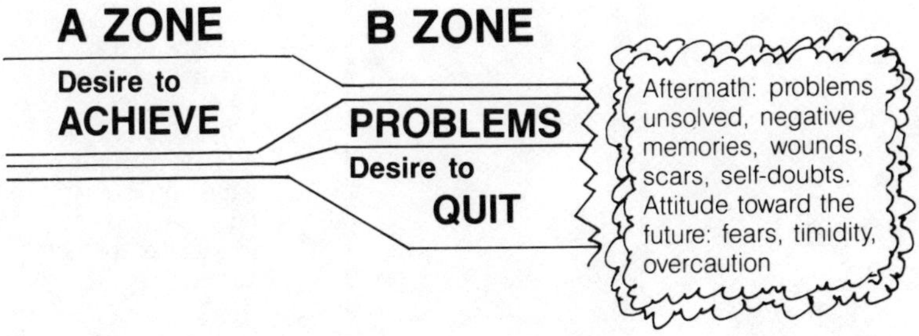

You could say this last chart illustrates the story of either Mr. Fatso in the office or the marathon runner! It also illustrates the story of Rehoboam, who, when his father King Solomon died, ascended to the Israelite throne at the height of Israel's greatest glory. He had everything going for him, but with the first challenge to his leadership, he crumpled.

Cut. The project was aborted. The kingdom split.

And there are those sad words of the Apostle Paul, in prison in his final days, when he wrote, "Demas has forsaken me, having loved this present world. . . ." Cut. That project aborted, too. And Demas is never heard of again.

But over the centuries millions have resisted dropping out; they've battled their difficulties and survived, and eventually—eventually, as surely as God is God—*C Zones emerged:*

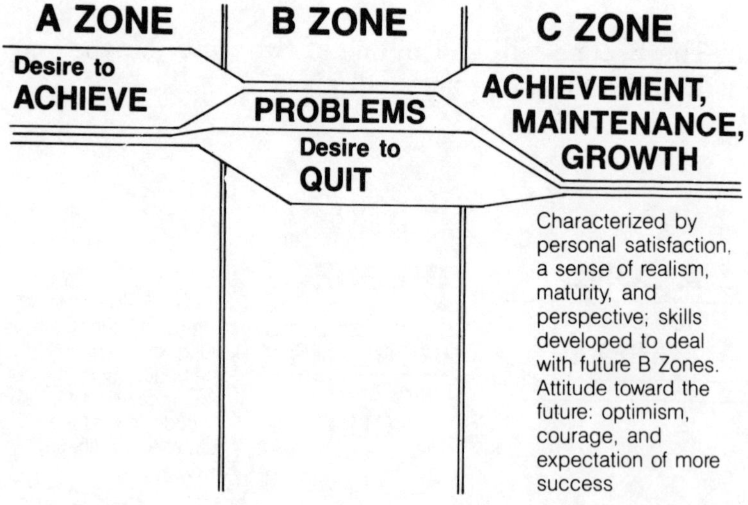

Recently we were counseling three young missionary women overseas: two short-termers (for two years each) and one on career status. All three were single. And all three had the same question: "How do you know when to quit?"

There were tears.

We talked about A, B, and C Zones. In certain areas of their lives all three were obviously in B Zones.

We said, "It may be that you'll 'quit' before your term of service is over. A short-termer may stick out two full years, but in her heart she quit six months early, or a year early, and she's just grinding it out until her time's up.

"She must ask God for ways to conquer, or at least come to terms with, each problem; she's got to solve each one or at least put it to rest in her mind—so that she can get into the C Zone *before her two years are over.*

"Only then," we said, "is she able to decide whether to terminate positively, with correct perspective on both the good aspects and the bad, or decide to continue.

"Pray for answers to the things that bug you," we said. "These things don't have to be chronic—at least in your mind. They don't have to keep you miserable forever. Go after solutions! Expect relief! Expect a C Zone to come—not in escaping, but in this very job, in this situation, with these people. Ask God for it!"

In the silence they were thoughtful.

Then Karen said, "It's easy these days to make short commitments—two years here, three years there—without any sense of great satisfaction and achievement."

"That's because," we said, "so many never get past their B Zones, so they're not moving forward, they're moving sideways from one thing to another—with all their fears and uncertainties still clinging to them."

"What a need there is to commit ourselves to one thing and stick it out until we really succeed at it!" exclaimed one of them. *(Begin, persevere, win!)*

"Staying power," we murmured. "We're writing a book. . . ."

"By
perseverance
the snail
reached
the
ark"

—Charles Haddon Spurgeon (1834–1892)

C H A P T E R 3

Don't Look Back, Look Forward

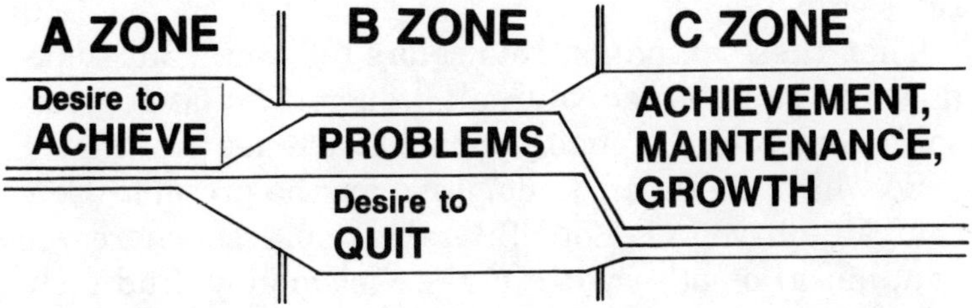

There's the preacher out on the golf course who played the worst round of his entire life.

"I quit! I quit!" he screamed.

His friends were horrified. "George, just because of one lousy day, you wouldn't give up your golf altogether?"

"Not my golf," he heaved, "the ministry!"

B Zones can get you completely out of control. That's why you need first to back up and get a good general look at where it is you've come from and where you're headed.

We all need perspective. Mentally climb a tree and study the whole view of your life, horizon to horizon. It should give you cause for great optimism.

Humanism tells you you're shaped by your past, that however your mother buttoned you up determined how you are today. How discouraging! How damaging! Humanism says that your past—your ancestors, your history, your early environment, everything people "did to" you when you were young and helpless—all that past has determined your "script," and it's the only script you have.

And you can't change it. It's the old thing about shutting the barn door after the mule is out. Or as Charles E. Wilson puts it, "It's futile to talk too much about the past—something like trying to make birth control retroactive!"

Then these humanist counselors tell you, "But somehow you can change yourself; you *must* change yourself." And you're probably too disheartened even to try.

So what's there left to do? Live for the present. (Concentrate on your B Zone!!) Grab happiness where you can, moral or otherwise; make fast money; find techniques for instant success—"eat, drink, and be merry, for tomorrow we die."

Kierkegaard described modern man as a prisoner in a dungeon condemned to be executed the following morning: "You'd think he'd be concerned, but no, he spends his last moments playing cards."

God's Word gives a completely different picture.

> You are, in truth, being shaped by your future. And the more you believe in that future, keep your eyes on it, and move toward it, the more strongly it will influence and shape you.

If only the two of us had seen that principle in the B Zone of our marriage! We got discouraged because we were looking backward at our A Zone, which was of course better, and we supposed the rest of our marriage would be more B Zone. Nobody told us about the C Zone which was coming! How it would have encouraged us—yes, and even shortened the difficult era!

Think about Job. Caught in a really bad B Zone, he could only look backward:

> How I long for the months gone by,
> for the days when God watched over me. . . !
> Oh, for the days when I was in my prime, . . .
> when the Almighty was still with me
> and my children were around me (Job 29:2–5).

Job's three friends didn't help him a bit. But at last another fellow came along, Elihu, who *looked from Job's B Zone to his coming C Zone* (nobody else had thought of that) *and so offered Job hope.* He said,

> [God] is wooing you from the jaws of distress to a spacious place free from restriction, to the comfort of your table laden with choice food (Job 36:16).

He turned out to be fabulously accurate. God was wooing Job! And when Job had learned all the lessons he was supposed to learn, God ended his B Zone and moved him on to "a spacious place free from restriction, / to the comfort of [a] table laden with choice food."

The two of us read that verse when we were going through a lulu of a B Zone, two years of unrelieved threat of financial calamity.

"He is wooing you," we read, "from the jaws of distress. . . ."

("Lord," we cried, "the jaws are closing!")

". . . to a spacious place free from restriction. . . ."

We connected this promise with others:

> He reached down from on high and
> took hold of me;
> he drew me out of deep waters. . . .
> He brought me out into a spacious
> place (Ps. 18:16, 19).

You have not handed me over to the enemy
but have set my feet in a spacious place (Ps. 31:8).

For you, O God, tested us;
  you refined us like silver.
You brought us into prison
  and laid burdens on our backs.
You let men ride over our heads;
  we went through fire and through water,
  but you brought us to a place of abundance
(Ps. 66:10–12).

Maybe Job pictures us all more than we have realized. We all suffer, we all struggle, we all ask why—and *when we see God,* we will all come out into a "spacious place free from restriction, / to the comfort of [a] table laden with choice food."

You, like us, have "Job experiences." You get hassled until it doesn't seem worth hanging on. We'd like to be your Elihu, to help give you hope—and staying power.

Hear it again: *The more you believe in your future, keep your eyes on it, and move toward it, the more strongly it will influence and shape you.*

Start training your mind to look up and look beyond, to see God and to see your future, to get both faith and hope.

Get tough! Endure! Eyes forward!

Hang on and don't let go!

Begin, persevere, win!

Forgetting those things which are behind [wrote the Apostle Paul] and reaching forward to those things which are ahead, I press toward the goal for the prize of the upward call of God in Christ Jesus (Phil. 3:13–14).

In the midst of struggle, when you remember what's coming, you feel hope. Hope lifts and exhilarates. It expands your lungs and redoubles your energies. The hassles of the present seem easier.

The two of us recently watched the Los Angeles Lakers sweating out final games for the NBA (National Basketball Association) championship. Toward the end, as the Lakers began to realize more and more that winning was likely, bruises and fatigue were forgotten. Glory was coming. Rest and play were coming. Family times were coming. Whopping bonus checks were coming. You could see it on their sweaty faces.

Think about your long-term future as a Christian. No wonder it's called "the blessed hope"; it's breathtaking! You'll see Christ face to face. You'll be like Him. You'll be free from sin; you'll have a perfect body; you'll inherit all that Christ inherits. You'll at last be perfectly fulfilled, complete, whole, and in perfect union with God.

Says Israeli scientist Shlomo Breznitz,

> Hope—if it is serious, if it is long-term—leads to physiological changes that can improve the body's resistance. In our studies we have found two hormones—*cortisol* and *prolactin*—that are strongly affected by an attitude of hope. While we don't know the precise links, the evidence points to a strong relationship between such neurochemicals and the immune system. . . .
>
> People with a strong faith, whether from religious beliefs or just good experience with trust, are the ones who stick it out in the worst circumstances.[1]

"There is no medicine like hope," writes O. S. Marden, "no incentive so great, and no tonic so powerful as expectation of something tomorrow."[2]

1. Shlomo Breznitz, director of the Ray D. Wolthe Centre for the Study of Psychological Stress, University of Haifa, Israel. Quoted by Dr. Daniel Goldman in *American Health,* December 1984, 80 Fifth Ave., New York, N.Y. 10011.

2. Lawrence J. Peter, *Peter's Quotations* (New York: Bantam Books, by arrangement with William Morrow and Co., 1977), p. 248.

Wasn't it a stroke of genius on the part of God to set us up a tremendous C Zone and let us know it's coming?

Says Romans 8:18–19,

> The sufferings of this present time are not worthy to be compared with the glory which shall be revealed in us. For the earnest expectation of the creation eagerly waits for the revealing of the sons of God.

Time magazine recently contained an essay called "Hope Sprouts Eternal," in which it commented that without the power of hope,

> the world would be quite a different place. Christopher Columbus would probably have looked to the Western horizon and told his crew, "There doesn't seem to be anything in sight. Let's turn around and go home."
>
> Military campaigns would have ended differently. George Washington, surveying his ragged forces at Valley Forge, would have surrendered. So would Winston Churchill in the early days of 1941. The march of industrial technology would have zigzagged. Thomas Alva Edison, after spending $40,000 to test umpteen hundred possible filaments for an electric light, would have shrugged and said, "I give up. Nobody will ever figure this out."
>
> Most of the heroes of literature would have been far less heroic. Romeo would have said to Juliet, "You're a real neat girl, but I don't think our families are ever going to let us get married. Maybe we should split up." Captain Ahab would have given up whaling and retired to grow petunias in a suburb of New Bedford.[3]

Hope is a powerful stimulant. Dr. Viktor Frankl, an Austrian psychiatrist, was interned in a concentration camp in World War II, and he studied who survived such camps and who didn't. He said it really wasn't a matter of who was healthiest or strongest—it was whether they

3. *Time* magazine, January 28, 1985, p. 92.

had a girl back home waiting for them or some vocational goal they dreamed of realizing![4]

And hope is God's gift to you to keep you healthy and positive and persevering. That light at the end of your tunnel isn't a train, it's your fabulous C Zone, and you need to strongly orient yourself to it!

The more you believe in that future—hear it once more—*the more you keep your eyes on it and move toward it, the more strongly it will influence and shape you.*

And in your immediate life here on this earth, your dreams, your projections, your goals, your longings—or your lack of them—are strongly influencing the present you.

If you're reminiscing too much, you're dying.

Eyes ahead. Forward march. Is there a river before you? Wade in. The cold current will galvanize your bones. A mountain beyond the far bank? Move on. Move up . . . up . . . up . . .[5]

4. Viktor Frankl, *Man's Search for Meaning* (New York: Pocket Books, 1975).

5. James Hefley, *Life Changes* (Wheaton, Ill.: Tyndale House, 1984), p. 178.

You will only
discover excellence
on the other side
of hard work

CHAPTER 4

Begin!

A ZONE

Desire to ACHIEVE

Characterized by idealism, perhaps naivete, and maybe also apprehension. Attitude toward the future: hope for success

Whatever you want to do in your life, you can't do it until you begin.

Back to our writing. We had this book to do, and we'd been gathering material for almost two years. Our files were full of hundreds of quotes and book references and Scriptures and ideas jotted on notebook pages and scraps and scraps of paper!

But gathering material doesn't write a book.

We had to block off time in our date book, hole up in a friend's condo away from interruptions, and sit down and *begin*. We wrote and wrote, and it was pretty bad. We showed it to our son Nels, and he thought it was bad, too. We wrote some more, we read each other's stuff, we talked it through, and then we wrote again. It was several weeks before the juices began to flow and there was anything at all decent, finishable, on paper. Beginning isn't easy.

But there never would have been a book if we hadn't *begun*. Until we put words on paper, whether good or bad, we had nothing to work on, nothing to improve, nothing to throw out!

Whatever you want to, you can't do it until you begin. (Don't wait until you're not tired. Everybody is usually tired. And don't wait until you have more time. People seldom have enough time. Understand all that, and get on with what you dream of doing.)

You want to lose weight? *Begin.*

You want to read through the Bible? *Begin.*

You can't do anything until you begin! Developing staying power comes later in the B Zone; first you have to begin. You worry you won't finish? You won't finish anything at all unless you first begin!

> Whoever watches the wind will not plant;
> whoever looks at the clouds will not reap (Eccles. 11:4).

Begin!

What is it God created you to do in your life? He's had projects in mind for you since the beginning of time, which no one can complete but you. You are God's "workmanship, created in Christ Jesus to do good works, which God prepared in advance for [you] to do" (Eph. 2:10). It's time for you to start fulfilling them.

Said the Lord to Jeremiah,

> Before I formed you in the womb I knew you,
> before you were born I set you apart; . . .
>
> Do not say, "I am only a child." You must go to everyone I send you to and say whatever I command you. Do not be afraid of them, for I am with you and will rescue you (Jer. 1:5–8).

Wally Rippel was a very young Cal Tech graduate student when he wandered into our church on a Sunday morning and accepted Christ as his Savior. The next Thursday he sat in class looking out a window at smog-filled air, and the thought came to young Wally, *Lord, is one of the reasons you made me, to help clean up this dirty brown air in Your beautiful world?*

It was Wally's commissioning, and it was a life-changing moment. Eventually Wally electrified an old Volkswagen bus and challenged MIT in Cambridge to build its own electric car for a coast-to-coast race. When Wally's car won, it was placed in the Smithsonian Institution. These days Dr. Wally Rippel, more than ever a warm-hearted, growing believer in Christ, is an important part of this world's battle for clean air.

That's Wally's project; what's yours? The same God who created Wally created you; and He has unique, specific plans just for you.

Then ask Him to show you what they are. That's not simplistic; that's utterly practical. He formed you to be His school teacher or His bank president or His janitor or His diplomat, for glorious, unique, strategic reasons.

A Zones are clean; they're fun; they have no bad memories, only future hopes. But how do you know you're entering the right one?

Don't be too dogmatic about what God "told" you to do. People have thought that God was telling them to do a lot of kooky things, about which God must be scratching His head and saying, "I said *what?*"

The two of us remember a young man who came to our church for quite a while, who declared God had called him to witness to Hollywood movie stars. But through the months, as he gave reports and hoped we would take on his support, his only information about them seemed to be what he read in movie magazines, and his only "contacts" with them were letters he wrote which got no answers. We began thinking God must really have called him to do something else, and he wasn't listening.

We are fallible. We don't always hear well. What God may be trying to say to us can be subtly mixed in our minds with what we want to hear. Nevertheless,

> As a father has compassion on his
> children,
> so the LORD has compassion on
> those who fear him;
> for he knows how we are formed,
> he remembers that we are dust (Ps. 103:13–14).

He is not despising you. And if you sincerely do want His will, He will not play coy with you. He will let you know—through circumstances, through the counsel of godly people, and most of all through your quiet, intimate fellowship with Him in the Word and in prayer.

1. *Begin with prayer.* Jesus began His earthly ministry with prayer (see Luke 3:21).

He began His small group of disciples in prayer (see Luke 6:12–13).

He launched His experience of the cross in prayer (see Luke 22:39–44).

The whole church was born in prayer (see Acts 1:14). Seek God's mind from the start.

2. *Define as specifically as you can what you're about to do.* If there are steps in the process, rank them in order of importance. What will be the cost of each step and of the whole, in money, in time, in emotional energy, in manpower?

> Which of you, intending to build a tower, does not sit down first and count the cost, whether he has enough to finish it (Luke 14:28)?

3. *Tell several people close to you what you hope to do:* your spouse, your best friends, your small group. Don't

tell the world at large; you haven't done it yet. But you need the accountability and prayer support of a special few.

4. *Begin some little part of your project immediately.* Even a small step is a step. And if possible, do something toward your project every single work day, to keep it always before you.

5. *Give yourself deadlines, and let your supporters know your deadlines.* Both the prayer and the pressure will be great motivators! But if you miss a deadline or fail at a part of your project along the way, don't be too discouraged. Every process has both failure and success built into it along the way. Ted Williams, one of baseball's all-time best batters, failed six times out of ten in his best year when he batted .400!

Now, this next step is terribly important, and if it's followed, it will save many people from quitting at some future point:

6. *Anticipate all the troubles you can.* Be calmly realistic to know they're coming. Get ready for your B Zone.

> A sensible man watches for problems ahead and prepares to meet them. The simpleton never looks, and suffers the consequences (Prov. 27:12 TLB).

Whatever your project—including the "project" of living the Christian life—make all the preparations you can to get ready for your B Zone.

You're not
finished
until you think
you are

C H A P T E R 5

Whatever Your Situation—"Stick It Out till June"

When Nels was in early high school, he wasn't applying himself and studying well. Having lunch one day with a friend, we were telling her how we were going bananas over our happy, unstructured, unmotivated, and unconcerned boy.

"I know what you mean!" said Marian. "Our Johnny was exactly the same. I don't think he ever would have turned out so well if we hadn't sent him to Stony Brook."

Stony Brook! We knew that fine Christian school outside New York City, and we asked Nels if he'd like to go. He was thrilled. Fifteen-year-old Nels dreamed of the glamour of an Eastern prep school and of wowing them with his personality and his tennis. . . .

It took him about a week to get thoroughly homesick. He decided that he was a true California beach boy and that from September to Christmas certainly ought to be as long as anyone should endure the East Coast.

Boy, did we have phone bills! He kept begging to come home at Christmas to stay, and we kept telling him he must complete that one school year.

"Nels," we said, "if you want to finish high school in California, we will love having you at home. But you really must stick out Stony Brook until June. You don't want to remember this as the year you were a quitter."

At Christmas he came home. He'd had a deep cold for

three months, he was unbelievably skinny, and his face was all broken out. He looked terrible.

And he announced he'd sold his furniture, given up his dorm room, told everybody good-bye, and shipped home all his belongings.

"Well," we said, "we love you, Skipper, and when you're gone we miss you terribly, but you'll have to pay to ship your things back again. And you can just do without room furnishings until June."

He couldn't believe us! We said, "We don't want to spoil Christmas by arguing. Let's not talk about it until the Monday after Christmas, okay? Then we'll go spend the day in the desert and talk and pray together."

On December 29 the three of us drove to Palm Desert. By the end of the day Nels knew he'd lost, and it's a wrenching thing to see a skinny, six-foot-one lad cry. We sat there watching in agony as he paced back and forth in the sunshine he loved, and then he ended the discussion like this:

"All right, Mom and Dad, I'm going back. I hate it; I don't want to go, but you guys are forcing me."

(He wiped his runny nose with his hand, and when he heaved an uncontrollable sob, it just tore us apart.)

"But I just want you to know one thing. Even though I'm going back and I don't want to, we still love each other, and nothing is ever going to change that!"

Can't you believe how we were absolutely melted and how our hearts went out to him?

At that moment, and through the next six months, we prayed night and day for our dear boy. His cold continued to go in and out of pneumonia until spring, and he never did well scholastically. But can you imagine how continually and intensely we prayed over our dear, skinny, fragile, fifteen-year-old Nels? *He had surrendered himself in love to our will, and because of that he was in a distant and (to him) difficult place.*

"Lord," we prayed day and night, "ease his pain! Lord, give him godly friends! Lord, help him study! Lord, help him know we love him! Lord, help him see how those dear teachers and staff are on his side! Lord, dry up his cold! Lord, turn his thoughts to you! Lord, strengthen and help our dear boy! Lord, comfort him! Lord, help the time pass quickly until he's home!"

With April and May came thawing and more sunshine and more tennis, and Nels began to like it a little better. By June he was glad he'd stuck out the year, and by midsummer, at home, he had trouble deciding whether to go back and finish high school at Stony Brook.

He didn't—but he tells us that year was his most necessary and most life-changing year so far. We know it; we see it.

A little epilogue to the story came several years later when the three of us were dining in a local restaurant. Nels, rested, handsome, happy, and growing up, commented, "Mom and Dad, look across the room. There's ______, who went back East to school the same fall I did and dropped out at Christmas time. Boy, I'm so glad I don't have to look back on that year and remember myself as a quitter."

* * * * *

And here you are, and here are the two of us—Jesus Christ's dear, fragile, immature kids. Our schooling is in a difficult place, and we're far from our heavenly home. *But we've surrendered ourselves in love to His will—and don't you think that melts Him?* Don't you think His heart goes out to us? Don't you think that makes Him intercede for us continually and intensely, "with groans that words cannot express" (Rom. 8:26)?

See from the book of Hebrews that—

1. *He sympathizes with you.* (He's not looking down on you ready to belt you one with a big stick.)

For we do not have a high priest who is unable to sympathize with our weaknesses, but we have one who has been tempted in every way, just as we are—yet was without sin. Let us then approach the throne of grace with confidence (4:15–16).

2. *He is right there to help.* (And He's far more able to help than California parents with a son in New York.)

Because he himself suffered when he was tempted, he is able to help those who are being tempted (2:18).

3. *And He can bring you through in triumph.*

Therefore he is able to save completely those who come to God [the verb means "who make a habit of continually coming to God"] through him, because he always lives to intercede for them (7:25).

Friend, whatever your tough situation is right now—
Stick it out till June.

A diamond
is a piece of coal
that stayed
on the job

CHAPTER 6

Persevere!

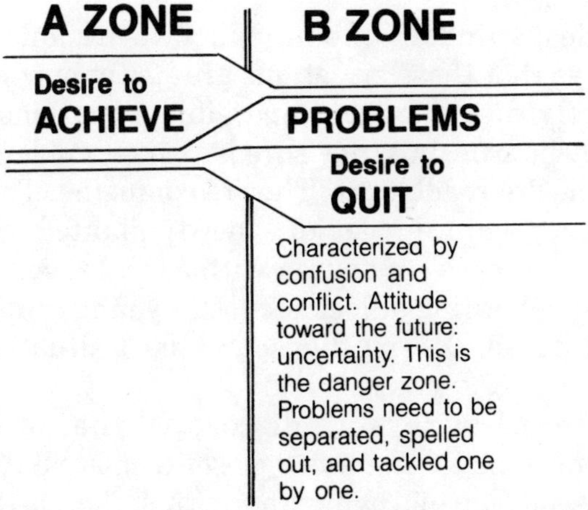

Do you relate to any of these situations?

1. "I've always been generous with my business partner, and he has just done me in."

2. "I hear people say they live victoriously over their own sexual desires, but I feel constantly defeated."

3. "I've never worked harder to market my product, and the sales have never been lower."

4. "I've asked God for the same thing every day for years, and He still hasn't answered."

5. "Just when I seemed to be getting on better with my spouse, we had another blowup."

6. "I serve at church as well as I know how, but still I get criticized."

7. "Just when it seemed I could finally afford a house, interest rates went up again."

8. "I've been socializing with this group for a long time, and I still feel I'm on the outside."

9. "When I'm honest in my business, my competitors do twice the volume."

10. "I'm tired of being the only one around here really committed and faithful. Nobody else seems to care, so why should I?"

Charles Swindoll, one of your favorite authors and ours, says that these situations are "great opportunities brilliantly disguised as impossible situations." Well, that may be true, but they sure look like problems, don't they? They're roadblocks. They're confusing. They hurt.

Not long ago we went to a newly planted church to have a conference—a church with a bright, godly young pastor shepherding a flock of mostly young couples with small children. Doesn't that sound like a situation full of the promise of success?

Within a few days we discovered that of the two church musicians, one was a closet homosexual and the other was declaring bankruptcy; that the pastor's wife was deeply scarred from a horrible childhood; that one of the few "mature" women in the congregation was going home from one of our evening meetings to kick out her husband of thirty years; and that another woman's teenage daughter had been missing for more than eleven months.

Talk about problems! We wondered if Satan would so thoroughly distract and discourage those people that they'd never have the emotional or spiritual energy to put a church together. The young pastor might well have wondered, too.

It reminded us of Nehemiah's project to put up

Jerusalem's wall—with problems coming so thick and fast, they were almost like too many mosquitoes to swat.

Is your life like that right now? Or does it get that way sometimes? So does ours.

Let's divide our suggestions into attitudes and actions.

A. Attitudes

1. *Develop an attitude of patience.* When you get going in a project and problems crop up, don't assume the project is wrong.

Jesus told about a fellow whose fig tree hadn't borne any figs for three years, so he told his gardener to cut it down. (That's the latest thinking: If something isn't "working for you," junk it.)

But the gardener was like God—long-suffering before the final judgment! "'Sir,' he replied, 'let it alone this year also, until I dig around it and fertilize it. And if it bears fruit, well. But if not, after that you can cut it down'" (Luke 13:6–9).

In other words, don't be hasty; don't quit too soon; what a shame if you destroy something that was going to get good.

Almost everything that's terrific today, earlier wasn't.

Any marriage.

Any church.

Any business.

Any person!

Any grape. Tomato. You name it.

Good things take time before they're good.

2. *Develop an attitude of trust.* God can change situations; His name is Deliverer. Then there are three possibilities for you:

One, He's just about to change your bad situation.

There was the Apostle Peter in prison—in perfect trust, asleep! Suddenly an angel got him up and led him to freedom (see Acts 12:3–11). Just like that.

Two, He'll change your situation later, but not yet. Lazarus, Jesus' dear friend, was dying. His sisters rushed Jesus the news. But Jesus lingered where He was two more days—indeed, letting Lazarus die (see John 11:6). His perfect plan wasn't to heal a sick man, but to raise a dead one.

God's timing is right. One of the most often-repeated commands in the Bible is to "wait on the Lord." Waiting on Him "grows you up"; it keeps your eyes off yourself and on Him; it gives you staying power.

Three, He doesn't plan to change your bad situation ever, as long as you live. Now, that's tough! How could God do that to you?

The Apostle John was exiled to the Island of Patmos, and it was just as cruel and needless as Peter's being thrown into prison. Have you seen Patmos? It's an ocean-surrounded *rock*.

John could have spent his time pacing that barren little beach, feeling bitter about what "they" did to him, and scanning the horizon every minute for a rescuer. But he didn't.

Quieted under the hand of God into a position of trust and receptivity, John received the most fabulous revelation of Jesus Christ and His future that any man has ever received, and as a result he wrote the Spirit-breathed book of Revelation.

Do you feel as if you're on a "Patmos" in your life? Are you feeling caught and trapped? Settle down. Look up. Let God decide whether He will act according to One, Two, or Three. For you, it will be perfect.

Friend, believe this: God will never let a B Zone last too long. Even if it ends in death, from eternity's viewpoint, it wasn't too long.

Said David Livingstone in Africa,

> Anxiety, sickness, suffering, or danger now and then, with a foregoing of the common conveniences of this life, may make us pause, and cause the spirit to waver and the soul to sink; but . . . only for a moment.
>
> I never made a sacrifice. Of this we ought not to talk, when we remember the great sacrifice which He made.[1]

And learn from Andrew Murray, who wrote,

> First, He brought me here; it is by His will that I am in this difficult place; . . . in that I will rest.
>
> Second, He will keep me here in His love, and give me grace in this trial to behave as His child.
>
> Third, He will make the trial a blessing, teaching me the lessons he intends me to learn, and working in me the grace He means to bestow.
>
> Fourth, in His good time He can bring me out again . . . how and when He knows.
>
> So . . . I am here by His appointment, in His keeping, under His training, for His time.

B. Actions

Now for the first suggestion for action.

Action 1: Pray. Jesus told His disciples "that they should always pray and not give up" (Luke 18:1). There's a clear demarcation here: You can choose between praying or quitting.

Then He tells a story to say that even *your prayers* must have staying power. He told about a woman who over and over brought her case before a judge, and he couldn't have cared less about her, but because *she bugged him*, he granted her request.

Jesus' reply was if an uncaring judge will say yes, how

1. Keswick Calendar, February 2, 1985.

much more will your Father, who loves you very much, say yes to you *who cry to him day and night* (v. 7)!

Another time—in fact, when the disciples said, "Lord, teach us to pray" (Luke 11:1)—Jesus taught them what to pray and how.

The "what" was the Lord's Prayer.

The "how"? With persistence. He told another story about someone who didn't care: this time somebody sleeping in bed who's asked by a friend at midnight (what lousy timing!) for some emergency food. The fellow says, "Don't bother me" (v. 7).

But the friend *bothers him anyway.* And Jesus says the fellow will say yes, *not* because of their relationship—that they're friends—but only because the guy keeps bugging him!

His conclusion: "If that uncaring friend in bed will say yes, how much more will your Father who loves you very much."

> So I say to you: Ask and it will be given to you; seek and you will find; knock and the door will be opened to you (v. 9).

In other words, "Come on, children, bug Me! Try it! Bug Me!"

In another place He says, "You do not have, because you do not ask God" (James 4:2). It's that simple.

It's the whole reason for B Zones, isn't it? Basically, life is not complicated. God knows we don't naturally turn to Him, so He lovingly jabs us with a pin. Then—

> The righteous cry out, and the LORD hears them;
> he delivers them from all their troubles (Ps. 34:17).

We should learn our lesson, shouldn't we? We should "get the point."

When a trouble jabs you, let your automatic reflex be prayer, serious prayer with staying power in it.

Action 2: Separate your problems, and deal with them one by one. What will help you keep your equilibrium, so you can conquer your difficult B Zone and move on? Be careful not to lump all your problems together into one big black cloud over your head and just say, "Poor me!" You must keep each problem separate in your thinking and attack them one by one.

Let's back up to that young pastor whose story opened this chapter. He could easily be overwhelmed by so many problems. He's got to think of them separately and attack them separately. For instance:

A. He might gently face the homosexual musician with two choices: to seek deliverance through repentance, counseling, and loving support—or to be fired. We would say his choice needs a specific, early deadline.

B. His dear wife's problem is an ongoing one, perhaps lifelong. She will always need from him large doses of affirmation and understanding, and perhaps she will need professional counseling.

C. He might make sure that the mother of the missing daughter and the musician facing bankruptcy each has a "small group" for emotional and prayer support. In the case of the musician, a member of that group could be assigned to monitor quietly and discreetly the need for funds in times of distress.

D. He might meet with the older couple, separately and together, to see if their marriage can be saved. If their problems are beyond his training, he could suggest a professional counselor. . . .

How do you swat mosquitoes? One by one.

You even delegate some swatting to other swatters, so your total attention isn't on the mosquitoes but on your project.

Moses processed Pharaoh's plagues one at a time and so got his people out of Egypt.[2]

2. See Outline 1 following this chapter.

Nehemiah dealt with opposition, workers' fatigue, unequal food distribution and so on, one problem at a time, and so built Jerusalem's wall.[3]

Says World Vision, "How do you feed a hungry world? One mouth at a time."

Don't leave any problem undealt with. Don't look the other way and pretend it isn't there. Don't thrash about trying to pinpoint blame. Don't be unrealistic in your assessment; maybe it's worse than you thought, maybe it's not as bad.

With the shock of a new problem, there will be a grieving process; expect it and go through it. Complain to the Lord, as David did in the psalms:

Deliver me from my enemies, O God; . . .
See how they lie in wait for me! (Ps. 59:1,3).

My companion attacks his friends;
he violates his covenant (Ps. 55:20).

I see violence and strife in the city.
Day and night they prowl about . . . (Ps. 55:9–10).

Talk every problem over thoroughly with the Lord; try writing down your prayers. It may help you (1) to digest thoroughly what has happened and (2) to be comforted by the One whose name is Comforter.

Action 3: Seek godly advice. Standing on the outside, others can see what you can't see, and they can offer creative solutions you haven't thought of.

Besides, the relational aspect is very important. Don't be alone with your problems; you need others now. Alone, you might think, *This problem proves the whole*

3. See Outline 2. For further Bible study, see also the outline of Job, Outline 3. The two of us outlined a period of our personal history as well (Outline 4). Want to try it yourself?

thing isn't working. It wasn't meant to be. I'm getting out.

Wise friends give other viewpoints. Was it a good thing to start with? Could it still be, if the problem weren't there? If the problem seems too big to conquer, can you coexist with it? Can you do an end run around it and reach your goal anyway?

Maybe the problem is with your job. If "digging your heels in" seems to be God's will, counselors will give you prayer support for that. Or maybe you need to retrench—go back to school for more training, attack your career another way. You may end up with a new skill or a new method or a new interest.

Loving friends have gathered around the two of us more than once to pray us through discouraging periods.

Jonathan once trekked to a forest to help his friend David find strength in God (see 1 Sam. 23:16–18); and David, encouraged, went on ultimately to become king.

Check your attitudes; check your actions. And keep moving forward.

Begin, persevere, win!

Outline 1

MOSES' PROJECT OF GETTING HIS FELLOW HEBREWS OUT OF EGYPT —— ENLARGES INTO → **PROJECT TO GOVERN THE ESCAPED HEBREWS IN RIGHTEOUSNESS**

A ZONE	B ZONE	C ZONE → A	B ZONE	C ZONE
DESIRE TO ACHIEVE	PROBLEMS DESIRE TO QUIT	ACHIEVEMENT, MAINTENANCE, GROWTH → DESIRE TO ACHIEVE ON A LARGER SCALE	PROBLEMS DESIRE TO QUIT	ACHIEVEMENT, MAINTENANCE, GROWTH (PROSPECT OF NEW A ZONE: CANAAN)
Exod. 3:1–5:1 Moses' call (3:1–4:17) so mixed with personal fears and doubts that project almost aborted before it got off the ground. Finally traveled to Egypt (4:18–26), linked up with Aaron (4:27–31), together made request of Pharaoh (5:1).	Exod. 5:2–12:30 Problems: Resistance of Pharaoh through ten plagues. Note as problems are handled one by one, Moses grows in confidence and stature (5:22–23; 6:12,30; 8:10,25,26; 9:30; 10:3,24,25; 11:6–8).	Exod. 12:31–51 Hebrews out of Egypt. Rules for living set for all escapees. Success in the first project has given Moses maturity, confidence, perspective, trust in God, skills for dealing with problems, and a new, larger vision: holiness for his people.	Exod. 13:1–33:23 Problems: Israelites' terror at Red Sea barrier, 14. Their grumbling over lack of water, 15; food, 16; Moses' leadership, 17. Attacked by enemies, 17:8ff. Threat of Moses' exhaustion, 18:17ff. Israelites' idolatry, 32:1ff. Tablets of law broken, 32:19. More rebellion through Leviticus, Numbers. Each problem dealt with one by one.	Exod. 34:1–Deut. 33:29 Permanent tablets of law given, 34:1ff. Tabernacle for worship ordained, planned, constructed, used, 35:4–40:38; more laws given in Leviticus, Numbers. Orderly census of population, Num. 1–4. Probing into Canaan, Num. 13. Second census, Num. 26. Moses' final words, Deut. 1:1–33:29 (Prospect of new A Zone: entering Canaan).

Outline 2

NEHEMIAH'S PROJECT OF REBUILDING JERUSALEM'S WALL — ENLARGES INTO — PROJECT TO GOVERN THE TRANSJORDAN JEWS IN RIGHTEOUSNESS

A ZONE	B ZONE	C ZONE	A ZONE	B ZONE	C ZONE
DESIRE TO ACHIEVE	PROBLEMS / DESIRE TO QUIT	ACHIEVEMENT, MAINTENANCE, GROWTH	DESIRE TO ACHIEVE ON A LARGER SCALE	PROBLEMS / DESIRE TO QUIT	ACHIEVEMENT, MAINTENANCE
1:1–2:18 Alerted to need, fasted, and prayed, not without his moments of fear and doubt, planned, traveled to Jerusalem, planned more, divulged his plans, gathered workers, began to build.	2:19–6:14 Problems: Increasing opposition from area Gentiles (2:19,20; 4:1–9; 6:1–14). Workers' fatigue (4:10). Workers' fear of opposition (4:11–23). Lowered morale because of inequity of food supplies; some growing richer at the expense of others (5:1–13). All these problems separately faced and dealt with, one by one. (Note as problems were handled, Nehemiah's growing self-confidence and stature: 2:2b, 4b, 17 18, 5:6, 7, 14–19; 6:11).	6:15 Wall completed. Rules for righteous living set for those living within its walls. Success in the first project had given Nehemiah maturity, perspective, skills in dealing with problems, and a new, larger vision: holiness for his people.		6:17ff. Problems: Spiritual confusion because Jews conformed to Gentile heathen enemies (6:17–19), then accommodated and even liked them (13:1–9, 28). Levites, priests not provided for (13:10–14). Sabbath violated (13:15–22). Intermarrying with Gentile idol-worshipers (13:23–31). All problems separately dealt with, one by one.	7:1–13:31 Orderly recording of population (chap 7). Revival! People clamored to hear God's Word (8:1–12), in obedience to it prepared the Feast of Tabernacles (8:13–18), mourned over their sins and prayed (chap. 9), made a covenant to obey the Lord (chap. 10), resettled to maintain and protect their city (11:1–12:26), worshiped (12:27–47).

Outline 3

"As you know, we consider blessed those who have persevered. You have heard of Job's perseverence and have seen what the Lord finally brought about. The Lord is full of compassion and mercy" (James 5:11).

Job's project: Righteousness (as far as he understood it) for self and family.

Sometimes problems are so great, success will not come without introduction of outside help.

Job's new project, righteousness for self, family, friends.

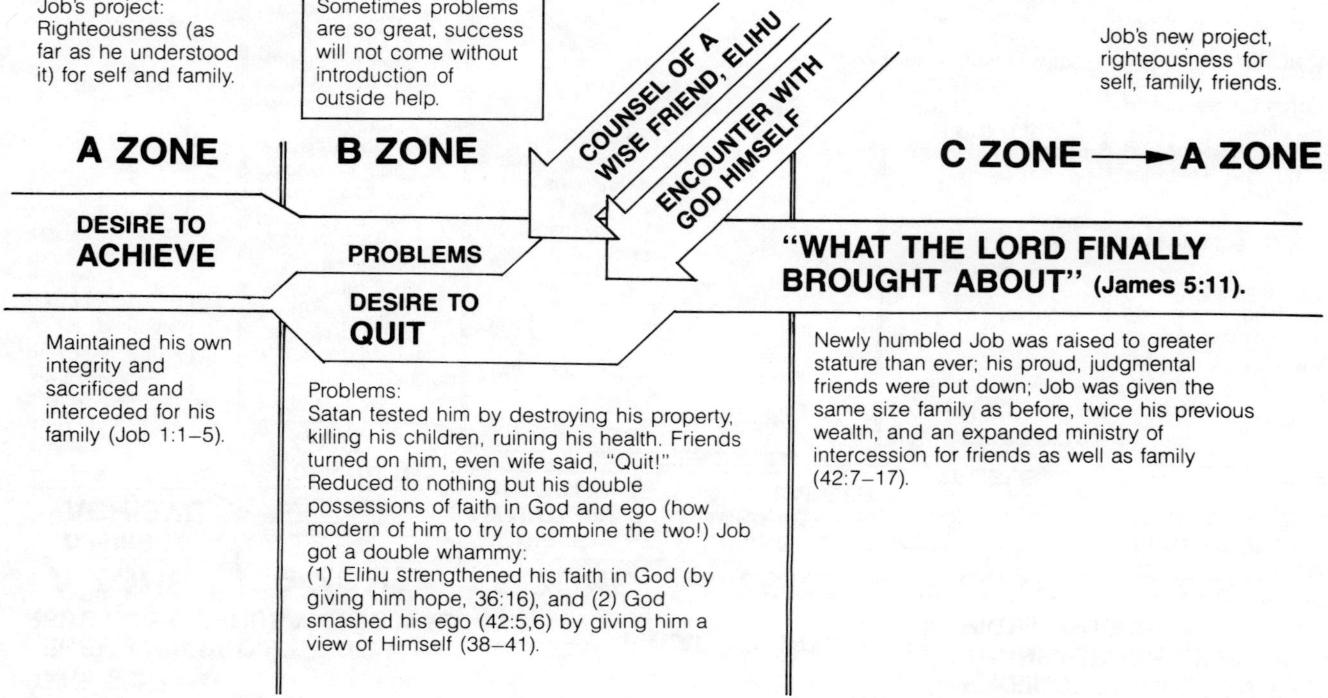

Maintained his own integrity and sacrificed and interceded for his family (Job 1:1–5).

Problems:
Satan tested him by destroying his property, killing his children, ruining his health. Friends turned on him, even wife said, "Quit!" Reduced to nothing but his double possessions of faith in God and ego (how modern of him to try to combine the two!) Job got a double whammy:
(1) Elihu strengthened his faith in God (by giving him hope, 36:16), and (2) God smashed his ego (42:5,6) by giving him a view of Himself (38–41).

Newly humbled Job was raised to greater stature than ever; his proud, judgmental friends were put down; Job was given the same size family as before, twice his previous wealth, and an expanded ministry of intercession for friends as well as family (42:7–17).

OUR TESTIMONY

Ray's project to get established as the young (35) pastor of a large (1,700 members at the time) church ——→ Enlarged into project (from defensive to offensive) to lead his people into revival and deeper righteousness

A ZONE	B ZONE	C ZONE	A ZONE	B ZONE	C ZONE
DESIRE TO ACHIEVE	PROBLEMS DESIRE TO QUIT	ACHIEVEMENT, MAINTENANCE, GROWTH	DESIRE TO ACHIEVE ON A LARGER SCALE	PROBLEMS DESIRE TO QUIT	ACHIEVEMENT, MAINTENANCE, GROWTH
YEARS ONE AND TWO Decisive call by the Lord and by the church, loving receptivity on the part of the congregation, children (12, 11, 10) adjusted well to schools, church went on radio locally and overseas, newspaper column and dial-a-phone ministry begun.	YEAR THREE Problems: Opposition began to arise from extremists, questioning Ray's Communist leanings because of Princeton Seminary and Presbyterian background. Letter circulated to all members, all missionaries. Anne and Ray called before Board of Deacons. Attendance, giving, membership declined. Atmosphere of malaise. Problems dealt with by prayer.	YEARS FOUR AND FIVE Opposition began melting away. Spirit of confidence gradually began to return. Growing feeling that Ray, approaching 40, was "our pastor." Success gave Ray perspective, skills in handling problems, and a new larger vision: holiness for his people.	YEAR SIX Numerical growth. Second morning service begun. Much quality leadership attracted to church and healthy conversion rate. Youth, missions, giving strengthened.	YEARS SEVEN TO TWELVE Campus enlarged, many building "growing pains." Occasional doctrinal questions (i.e., charismatic gifts, verbal inspiration of Scriptures). Leadership fatigue. Church employee growth from a handful to over sixty. Third morning service.	YEARS THIRTEEN TO TWENTY Churchwide revival which lasted for years. Ray's speaking ministry broadened to worldwide, with strong prayer support at home base. Times of congregation-wide "waiting on God." Music, missions, young adult—every area of church life strengthened. "Three priorities" became the daily lifestyle of several thousand of the church members.

"Perseverance
is not a long race;
it is
many short races
one after
another"

—Walter Elliott, *The Spiritual Life* (Paulist Press). "Quotable Quotes," *Reader's Digest*, June 1985

CHAPTER 7

Learn How to Be Hurt

George Verwer said that first. Get more familiar with pain, and don't let it be such a big deal.

The Apostle Peter, who eventually would be martyred, wrote his fellow believers,

> Dear friends, do not be surprised at the painful trial you are suffering, as though something strange were happening to you. But rejoice that you participate in the sufferings of Christ. . . . [As for instance, when you're honest in your business, your competitors do twice the volume.]
>
> However, if you suffer as a Christian, do not be ashamed but praise God that you bear that name (1 Pet. 4:12–13,16).

From prison, Paul wrote in Philippians 1:29—so calmly, so matter-of-factly!—"For it has been granted to you [these are God's gifts!] on behalf of Christ not only to believe on him, but also to suffer for him." You take one, you take the other.

This kind of attitude keeps you moving toward your goal. Negative circumstances aren't strong enough to detract you from the positive. Others may crumble; you keep going.

Look, suppose right now you hit your hand really hard on something sturdy nearby.

Does it hurt?

"Boy," you say, "that really stings."

Wait a minute. Does it still hurt?

"Yes," you say. "I can still feel it."

Think about that hurt. Concentrate on it. If you do, you'll feel it for quite a while.

Now what if you saw your only little daughter out in the street just about to get run over by a car, and in the nick of time you grabbed her from the car's path, but in so doing you hit your hand—as hard as you hit it just now.

Would it hurt?

You're smiling. "I wouldn't even be aware of it," you say, "I'd be so thrilled that my daughter was safe."

Exactly.

Living is between your ears. You can develop your own high pain threshold by concentrating on what's important and wonderful.

Paul said about his hardships,

> But *none of these things move me,* neither count I my life dear unto myself, so that I might finish my course with joy, and the ministry, which I have received of the Lord Jesus, to testify the gospel of the grace of God (Acts 20:24 KJV, emphasis added).

You're no martyr when you ignore pain to choose the joy of exciting accomplishment! That's *learning how to be hurt.*

We have a dear Indian friend who has two little sons with cystic fibrosis, such a rare disease that these are the only two known cases in all of India. It's fatal; his only other son has already died from it. Indian heat is the worst possible climate for it, and watching this loving man and his wife giving themselves day and night to these suffering boys is wrenching.

Do they have to stay in that heat? By no means. He's a brilliant researcher in nuclear medicine, whom the United Nations has consulted on such matters, and he gets offers to do important scientific work while living with high pay in cool places.

Then what holds that little family in sweltering South India? This: The rest of India is desperate for Christian Indian evangelists (foreign Christian workers are largely barred from the country), and this scientist uses his royalties and speaking fees to run a school to train evangelists who spread the Gospel all over that huge land.

What gives that family "staying power"—to stay in India? Here is their life verse:

> But none of these things move me, neither count I my life dear unto myself, so that I might finish my course with joy, and the ministry, which I have received of the Lord Jesus, to testify the gospel of the grace of God.

What about hurts in your life? What about past hurts? Do you hang onto them? A person may have hurt you only once—but every time you nurse and coddle that old grievance and concentrate on it, it hurts you again. Just like focusing on your stinging hand.

Why don't you have done with all that and start living?

Fix your eyes on Jesus (see Heb. 12:2). Does that sound like a cliché? Try it; it's revolutionary.

Jesus Christ is the Creator. He makes everything visible and invisible (see Col. 1:16)—including the events, people, and circumstances of your life. They're all His idea, and He has shaped them for one purpose: to make you holy. Each new pressure, irritation, pain, disappointment arrives not a moment too soon (when it would crush you) or too late (when it would be unnecessary). Each one is working for your good (see Rom. 8:28).

Then *quit reacting emotionally, and settle down.* Fix your eyes on Jesus, and develop a calm, tough optimism.

You can "be joyful always; pray continually; give thanks in all circumstances, for this is God's will for you in Christ Jesus" (1 Thess. 5:16–18).

And when suffering comes, you'll say, "Well, I'm not surprised. When I believed, I knew suffering was part of the package. No sense in becoming a dropout now; let's get on with what's important."

A curse on the false prophets who, when they're offering the Gospel to people, remove the warning label! They never mention the suffering part; they may even deny it; they play up only the benefits to get lots of converts.

Then when the new believers experience pain or trouble, they'll do one of two things: they'll reject Christianity altogether and become shaken, cynical, and harder to reach—or they'll last but they'll turn into weak, chronic whiners, focusing on their problems instead of on their purposes.

Realistic teaching, faithful to God's Word, produces realistic believers. Fix your eyes on Jesus—

> who for the joy set before him endured the cross, scorning its shame (Heb. 12:2).

Here's your model for ignoring pain. He scorned it; He belittled it "for the joy set before Him," so that before long He—

> sat down at the right hand of the throne of God (v. 2).

His C Zone was coming; He knew it; He could carry on with His great purposes and come out a winner.

> Consider him who endured such opposition from sinful men, so that you will not grow weary and lose heart (v. 3).

And understand this: from the large perspective, *pain has a very short life.*

> Therefore we do not lose heart. . . . For our light and momentary troubles are achieving for us an eternal glory that far outweighs them all. So we fix our eyes not on what is seen, but

on what is unseen. For what is seen is temporary, but what is unseen is eternal (2 Cor. 4:16–18).

This is an immutable principle of God. Look up Isaiah 54:7 and 8, and you'll see it:

> For a brief moment—B Zone;
> But with great mercies—C Zone.
> With a little wrath—B Zone;
> But with everlasting kindness—C Zone.

Think of the annual Jewish feasts. The mourning one (the Day of Atonement) lasted a day; the rejoicing one (the Feast of Tabernacles) lasted a week. That's God's style; that's His heart. "But," He says, "when it's time to mourn, children, *mourn.*"

A while back the two of us went through a really hard period, a time of frustration and depression, and by our own efforts there seemed no way out. We were in prison! Worshiping and praising God and telling each other "perspective, perspective!" seemed our only comforts.

Suddenly, when we were "sleeping," as it were, an angel struck us and said, "Quick, get up," and led us out through opened prison gates (see Acts 12:5–10). Not of our own doing we were free again, and the experience was behind us.

Christian in a B Zone, *every pain has a short life—but it needs to have its life.*

God could remove your hurt "right-this-minute-no-problem."

In an instant you're healed. (Perhaps He wants to do that.)

Or the one who's starting to bug you quickly moves out of town.

Or you hardly had time to feel a money pinch and you get a glorious raise.

God is powerful enough to do these "miracles." But did you profit enough from the trouble? Did it refine you?

Did it teach you the disciplines of patience, perspective, and trust?

A greater miracle might be your holiness.

Consider it pure joy, my brothers, whenever you face trials of many kinds, because you know that the testing of your faith develops perseverance. Perseverance must finish its work so that you may be mature and complete, not lacking anything (James 1:2–4).

A fellow was once watching a chrysalis emerging from a cocoon on its way to becoming a butterfly; and seeing it struggle, he felt sorry for it and clipped the cocoon to free it sooner. But nature's process had been cut short, and the butterfly was deformed.

Even Jesus, "Although he was a son, he learned obedience from what he suffered and, once made perfect, he became the source of eternal salvation" (Heb. 5:8–9).

Now one more final word about pain.

You get a breathtaking group photograph in Hebrews, chapter 11, of people of the past who trusted God. What a bunch! And the Lord certainly made some of them come out smelling like roses:

Noah was saved from the flood.

Once-childless Abraham was ultimately buried by his two sons.

Jacob ended up with wealth; Joseph, with power and fame.

And many more, through faith—

conquered kingdoms, . . . and gained what was promised; . . . shut the mouths of lions, quenched the fury of the flames, and escaped the edge of the sword; [their] weakness was turned to strength; [they] became powerful in battle and routed foreign armies. . . .

But—oh-oh, there were others. These others had lived just as valiantly as the first group. But they—

were tortured, . . . faced jeers and flogging, . . . were chained and put in prison. . . . were stoned, they were sawed in two; . . . were put to death by the sword. . . .

And when *you* trust God, in which group will *you* finish?

It's not for you or us to decide. Said Thomas à Kempis long ago, "He is not truly patient who will suffer only as much as he pleases or from whom he pleases."

Friend, let's calm down and toughen up. Let's develop staying power.

Without wincing, we must serenely say like Job in the midst of his troubles, "Though he slay me, yet will I trust Him" (Job 13:15 KJV).

Incidentally, after saying that, how did Job come out? Smelling like a rose.

"Our perseverance
is really
His perseverance
in us"

—James M. Baird, Jr.
Pastor, First Presbyterian Church,
Jackson, Mississippi

C H A P T E R 8

Will Your Dreams Come to Reality?

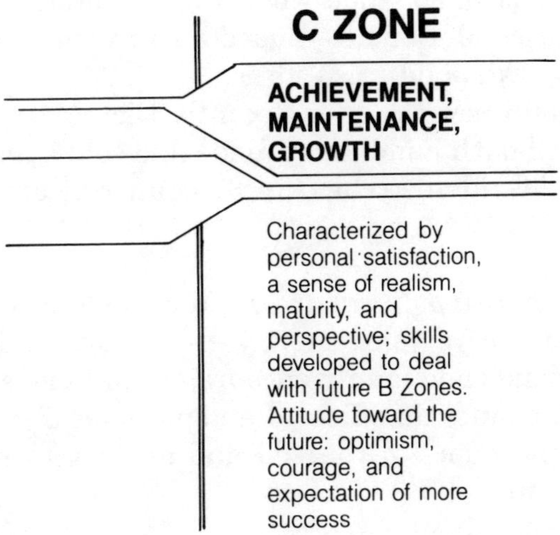
C ZONE
ACHIEVEMENT, MAINTENANCE, GROWTH
Characterized by personal satisfaction, a sense of realism, maturity, and perspective; skills developed to deal with future B Zones. Attitude toward the future: optimism, courage, and expectation of more success

You have a business dream. You have no reason to think God isn't in it, and you've got the desire, the talent, the time, the know-how, and the beginning capital.

So you launch it off its pad.

Soon everything begins to go wrong.

Should you duck out quickly and take your losses? Declare "Chapter Eleven"? Grab the remaining cash and flee to South America? Before you decide, think about this story.

In the 1940s, two brothers, Dick and Maurice, were

running a drive-in restaurant in the desert heat of San Bernardino, California. It had a lengthy menu and a lot of wasted food, so they got the idea of cutting the drive-in service and changing to a low-priced, assembly-line place with only favorite foods: burgers, fries, and drinks.

Everybody hated it. The snazzy carhops had left. People didn't like to wait on themselves. They didn't like to throw away their own trash. Dick says now that little eating place was a "complete disaster. There were times that we were tempted to throw in the sponge."

The turnaround came when the two brothers—Dick and Maurice McDonald—added a third partner named Ray Kroc, who had fresh ideas.

And you know the rest. Recently Dick McDonald ate the 50 billionth hamburger made and sold by his chain of 8,000 "Golden Arches" in 31 countries around the world.

Or you have a political dream. You feel God is motivating you to serve your country and make a difference. Godly friends and family encourage you to give it a try.

So you run for an office, at an enormous cost in time, money, and effort to yourself and to others who share your dream.

You lose.

Then what should you do? Let the dream die? Sell toothbrushes the rest of your life? Before you decide, think about this story.

A century ago a young fellow, aged 22, lost his job as a store clerk. The next year he became a partner in a small store, which failed. The next year he fell in love and courted the girl for four years, after which she said no. Later another sweetheart died.

At age 37, on his third try, he was elected to the state legislature, but two years later he lost the reelection.

At age 40, he was rejected for a political appointment. In this period he also had a nervous breakdown.

At age 41, his four-year-old son died.

At age 45, he was defeated for the Senate.

At age 47, he was defeated for vice president.

At age 49, he was again defeated for the Senate.

But at age 51, he was elected president of the United States. His name was Abraham Lincoln, and many consider him the greatest leader the United States has ever had.

Legitimate dreams are the wind in mankind's sails! Do you have visions and dreams of the future? The prophet Joel wrote that when the Holy Spirit is poured out on people, "old men shall dream dreams . . . [and] young men shall see visions" (Joel 2:28). Whatever your age, let the wind of the Holy Spirit motivate you, control you, and propel you along to the goals He's given you!

He gave Abraham a vision of his future in Genesis 12:2,3:

> I will make you a great nation;
> I will bless you
> And make your name great;
> And you shall be a blessing.
> I will bless those who bless you,
> And I will curse him who curses you;
> And in you all the families
> of the earth shall be blessed.

And time and again God reconfirmed these promises, to keep Abraham moving along toward their fulfillment.

God gave the Apostle Paul a vision of his future—that he would be God's "chosen instrument to carry [his] name before the Gentiles and their kings and before the people of Israel" (Acts 9:15). And that's exactly what Paul spent his life doing.

God put wind in Abraham's sails! He put wind in Paul's sails! And He can blow wind into your sails.

You have a dream, and you begin; you enter your A Zone. Your expectations are, with the passage of time, to get to C:

But barriers emerge:

What will you do?

The temptation is to drop out, to compromise, to forget C, to go to something less:

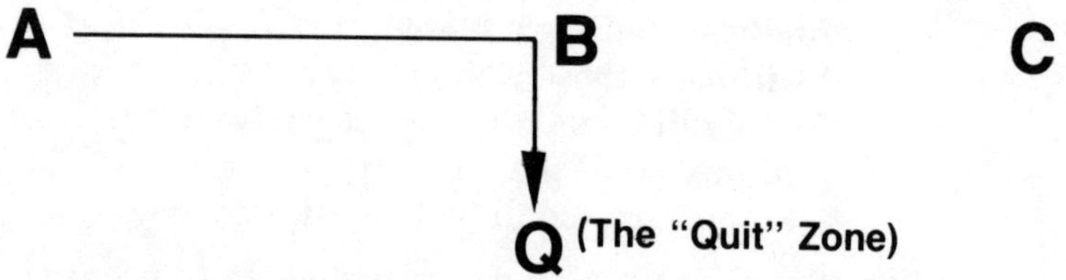

People do it every day. They say, "I couldn't do it"; "The weather was bad"; "I ran out of time"; "I ran out of money. . . ."

Dr. Robert Schuller names some of the excuses that lead down to the Q Zone. He says we drop out because of faces ("they won't let me"), farces (lies, prejudices), fences (limiting concepts), frustrations, fears, fatigue, faults of others, forecasts, and many more reasons.[1]

Four Observations About Quitting

When you're toying with the idea of giving up, along with all your other input, consider these facts:

1. *Everybody gets discouraged.* You're not at all alone.

A forlorn-looking Charlie Brown comes up to the information desk and asks, "Where do you go to give up?"

Jim Berkeley says a pastor can tell things are bad when . . . "he's elected Pastor Emeritus and he's only twenty-eight!"

2. *Everybody sometimes chooses the Q Zone.* Even the strongest get caught in a weak moment and give up on something. IBM recently quit its whole PCjr program. Sometimes bridges get only half-built. Space programs get scrapped. Still, the world goes on.

We say this to encourage you that the Q Zone isn't the end of everything. It is not the equivalent of hell! Sometimes it's even reversible.

3. *The Q Zone is very roomy.* There are lots of quitters in today's world. Some people quit and quit and quit. You can name plenty of low-pay jobs around you that are filled only by quitters; the jobs go on, but the faces are constantly new.

We ran into a quitter in a restaurant today. He's a handsome young single with a liking for women.

"What are you doing these days, Chip?" we asked.

"Oh, I was selling cars for a while," he offered. "Next month I'm going to Mexico for a couple of weeks."

"Mexico! Hey, hey! Business or pleasure?"

"Oh, just a little fun. . . ."

1. Robert Schuller, *Tough Times Don't Last, But Tough People Do* (Nashville: Thomas Nelson, 1983).

When we've asked him before, he's been learning to fly, or he's been waiting tables in a classy joint, or he's been going back to school, or he's been thinking about moving back East. . . .

When we see him again next year, he'll be trying out to teach tennis, or taking lessons to sell real estate, or chauffeuring some rich old lady. . . . But nothing lasts. And there's a different girl every time.

Chip keeps falling back into the Q Zone.

The Q Zone stays pretty full. Generally speaking, the people there are spending their (shortened) lives coddling themselves and dissipating. They're people full of fears—fears of the future, fears of their environment, fears of what others are "doing to" them. They get a pathetic little sense of achievement vicariously through the victories of others, but their self-images are still terrible. Their eventual end, after spending a lot of time accusing others and excusing themselves, is defeat and misery. Yes, the Q Zone is full of quitters.

4. *But you don't have to go there.* You may have been a quitter in the past, *but you are not now a quitter.*

We went to a seminar once where the speaker asked for smokers to raise their hands. One man raised his.

"But you're not a smoker," said the leader.

"Yes, I am," answered the man.

"When did you last smoke?" the leader asked.

"Just before the session," was the answer.

"Then," said the leader, "half an hour ago you were a smoker, but you're not at this moment.

"Now," he continued, "it's your choice, if you desire, to remain a nonsmoker for the rest of your life."

And we say to you, God is the God of new beginnings! "Now" is your fresh start. You are at this moment continuing to read this page, so *you are not a quitter.* And if you so desire, you can choose, one moment at a time from here on, to build into your life habits of commitment and staying power.

Begin, persevere, win!

Then your projects, your friendships, your marriage, your career will begin to develop this pattern:

Or this pattern:

Or this pattern:

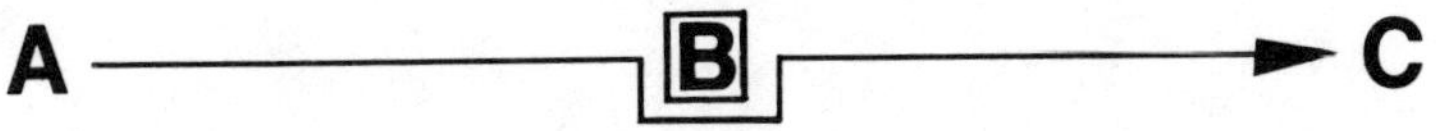

We heard about the terrible flood that came to Tooleysville one time, and one fella in his house was looking dismally out the window. Tooleysville looked like an ocean with buildings in it.

Then he noticed an amazing thing. A hat floated downstream, turned around and floated upstream again, turned and floated downstream, turned around and went up. . . .

"Hey, Mildred!" he called to his wife. "You won't believe this. Come look at that crazy hat!"

"Oh, that's Henry next door," said Mildred. "He swore come hell or high water he was going to get that lawn mowed this afternoon."[2]

2. "Laughter, the Best Medicine," *Reader's Digest,* March 1985.

If you're ever
tempted to give up,
just think of Brahms.
He took
seven long years
to compose his famous
"Lullabye."
Kept falling asleep
at the piano

—"Quip Trip" by Bob Orden,
American Way magazine,
April 16, 1985, p. 63

C H A P T E R 9

What Makes People Shipwreck Their Jobs

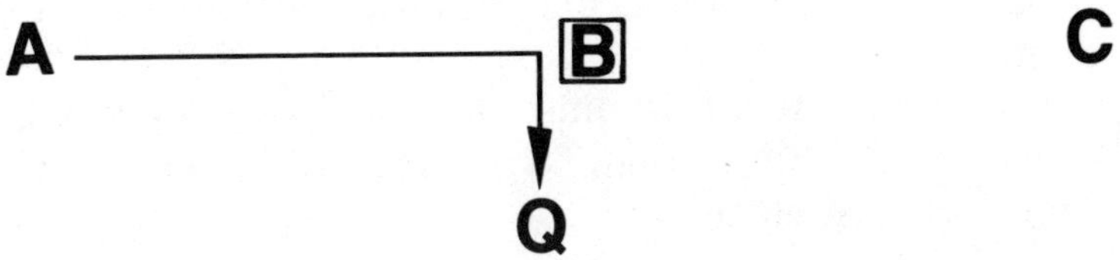

We're still remembering what Karen, our friend who's the short-term missionary, remarked: "It's easy these days to make short commitments—two years here, three years there—without any sense of great satisfaction and achievement."

"The switch is on," says *Newsweek* magazine. "A new generation makes career-hopping a full-time job."[1] It describes—

1. Virgil, who majored in political science, went on to business school, became a prep school teacher, tried social work and then journalism, now is a press officer at a university.
2. Craig, who quit a law firm where he made $50,000 a year, is now teaching history for $17,500 a year.
3. Alina, who also quit a law firm, spent two months as a fashion consultant, became a stock broker—and hasn't been happy with any of them.

1. "Ideas" section, *Newsweek* magazine, May 28, 1984, pp. 93–95.

4. Maurice, an investment banker, who quit and went to seminary and became an Episcopal priest, only to discover that the corporate model he thought he was escaping is also at work in the church.

But professional leapfrogging is becoming acceptable, say these switchers: "It's more like divorce. People have a right to ditch their misery."

What we said to Karen the missionary was that when many never conquer their B Zones but keep moving on, they're not moving forward, they're moving sideways—with all their fears and uncertainties still clinging to them.

They have initial dreams; they begin with great C Zones in view. But in their to-ing and fro-ing they'll seldom if ever reach them:

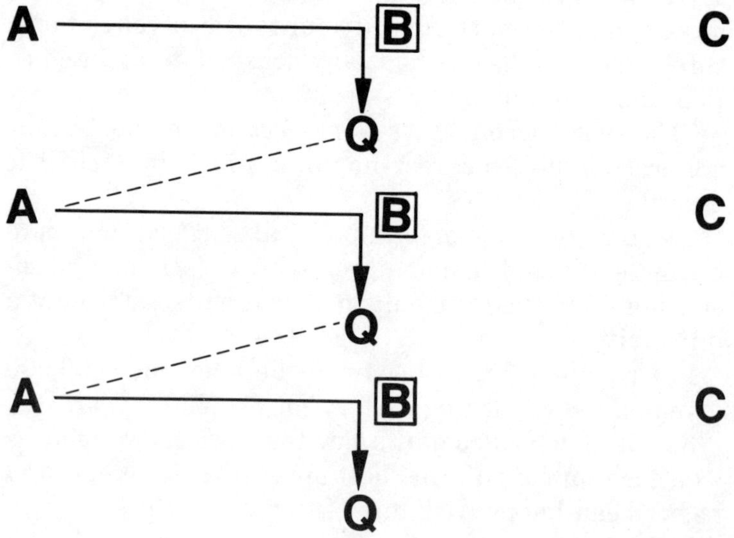

A Sunday school teacher asked her class if a leopard could change his spots. All the children shook their heads no except one little girl who nodded yes.

The teacher asked again if a leopard could change his spots, and again they shook their heads no except the same little girl who nodded yes.

The teacher asked what she meant by that, and the child said, "I don't know why a leopard who doesn't like his spot can't go to another one!"

Well, there must be a lot of leopards among American workers! In a recent twelve-month period a third of them (except for farm and home workers) transferred to something else. And a major denomination reports that the average stay of its pastors is now down to eighteen months.

Why do so many shipwreck their jobs? Here are some reasons:

1. *They develop an "entitlement mentality,"* which pushes them to ever-greater expectations (autonomy and "control" in their jobs, big pay, a view of the mountains or the water!).

Antidote: Let your first expectation be the ability of the Holy Spirit to do the best job possible through you.

> Settle down and earn the bread [you] eat (2 Thess. 3:12).

> Submit yourselves to your masters [or bosses] (1 Pet. 2:18).

> Obey your earthly masters . . . with sincerity of heart, just as you would obey Christ. Obey then not only to win their favor when their eye is on you, but like slaves of Christ, doing the will of God from your heart. Serve wholeheartedly, as if you were serving the Lord, not men (Eph. 6:6–7).

2. *They are quickly bored.* They want life to remain on a high pitch—sustain its hype—or they turn away to something else.

They change the channel.

They shut the book.

They find another church.

And lawyers become teachers, teachers become accountants, doctors and dentists go into real estate.

Antidote: Make your job challenging.

Why has God put you here? Are there people with whom you can share your faith, Christians with whom you can pray?

How can you improve in your work? What can you do to streamline the procedure and make it more efficient?

Write down your goals for this job, and each week do something to bring you closer to achieving them.

Critique your relationship with each person with whom you work. Are you encouraging them, affirming them? Is everything right between you? Do you need to mend any fences?

If you can, make your work area reflect you; make it fun for you. Can you put around mementos and pictures of family or friends? Can you add a little humor somewhere?

3. *They dream that the grass is greener on the other side of the fence.* Any B Zone is always more threatening than a new A Zone. Even the psalmist sighed, "O that I had the wings of a dove! / I would fly away and be at rest" (Ps. 55:6).

We read an article recently by a Vermont farmer who says, "Every cow, horse, sheep and goat I have known has spent much of its time trying to eat grass on the other side of the fences." They ram their heads through and get stuck, they push against fences until they bend them down, they creep under them or jump over them at every opportunity.

And when a neighboring farmer put bales of musty hay outside his cows' fence because they normally won't eat it—they only like the sweet grass inside—the cows formed a long row, heads through the fence, and eagerly chomped the musty hay. The neighbor figured they reasoned like this:

"That hay is out of our reach because he doesn't want us to have it. Therefore it must be exceptionally good. So even at the risk of tearing our necks on this wire, let's spend the rest of the day trying to steal it."

And that's just what they did.[2]

Career switchers are apt to leave behind unfinished jobs, disappointed employers, and broken dreams. But maybe in the new job they can at last find . . . musty hay?

Antidote: In almost all cases, conquer your B Zone before you move! Deal with the problems one by one; solve them or at least come to terms with them. Stay until you've attained a measure of success, you've completed a job phase, you've achieved a good record.

From the position of the C Zone, your transfer to something new could well be beneficial.

Do not be anxious about anything, but in everything, by prayer and petition, with thanksgiving, present your requests to God (Phil. 4:6).

Yes, it calls for a lot of fortitude.

It calls for a lot of saying no to quick ways out, when it would be easier to say yes.

Ann Landers says, "I know of no surgical procedure that will replace macaroni in the spine with a rigid backbone. This is strictly a do-it-yourself project."[3]

There was a time during World War II when American forces were pressed to the limit in Belgium. The place was Bastogne; the crisis was the famous Battle of

2. Noel Perrin, "The Grass Is Always Greener," *Reader's Digest,* August 1984, pp. 47, 48.
3. "Quotable Quotes," *Reader's Digest.*

the Bulge. American casualties were high, and the enemy seemed dominant.

Then on that fateful day in December of 1944, the Axis commander sent word to the Allied troops asking for their surrender.

Back went the message of Commanding Brigadier General A. C. McAuliffe in a famous, one-word reply: "NUTS!"

A father once said to his boy, "Son, you gotta set a goal and never quit. Remember George Washington?"

The son said, "Yes."

"Jefferson?"

"Yes."

"Abraham Lincoln?"

"Yes."

"You know what they all had in common?"

"What?"

The father said, "They didn't quit. Remember Ozador McIngle?"

The kid said, "No. Who was he?"

"See, you don't remember him. He quit!"[4]

4. Robert Schuller, *Tough Times Don't Last, But Tough People Do* (Nashville: Thomas Nelson, 1983), p. 202.

"*Press on.*
Nothing in the world
can take the place
of
persistence"

—Football coach Vince Lombardi.
Favorite quotation of Ray Kroc,
co-founder of McDonald's hamburgers

CHAPTER 10

Learn the Art of Midflight Refueling

Pace yourself. That's so important! A lot of people go to the Q Zone because of plain fatigue.

Do you picture staying power as just plodding uphill through one horrible situation after another, gritting your teeth, and hating it all the way?

Our bouncy, redheaded friend Marge wrote on the back of an envelope to us recently, "Eat your dessert first. Life is so uncertain."

Why not? Or at least nibble bites along the way. Pace yourself. Pick some daisies. Kick up your heels now and then.

Your job doesn't call for a full-fledged vacation except once a year? Then pace your work schedule with a thousand mini-vacations.

A while back the two of us were really tired. When we'd started Renewal Ministries several years before, we'd misjudged our schedules and overbooked. Now we were paying for it, racing from one conference to another and speaking as soon as we got off the plane, then racing home to pile into stacked-up correspondence and office work.

No vacations, not even days off. Well, we are revamping our schedule to try to pace ourselves better, but an immediate help was remembering what a lawyer friend of ours does. He doesn't take one vacation a year, he takes hundreds, usually one or two hours long. He adds them to his lunchtime, or he tacks them onto drives to see clients, or he may take an early morning one before he goes to the office.

He lightens his workload by building in brief respites along the way. Without quitting the journey, he refuels midflight.

Where does he go? What does he do? He explores. He prowls. He may visit a museum or an art gallery, or he may just open a door to see what's on the other side.

One day we said, "How about taking us on one of your vacations some lunchtime?"

Our friend's office is in downtown Los Angeles. In less than a week the three of us had started out reinvestigating some of his discoveries:

An old boxing gym, where greats used to spar and where has-beens still do.

A gorgeous Greek church.

One of L.A.'s oldest buildings, an architectural wonder open eight floors up, with an old iron elevator cage.

An international grocery mart.

He inspired us!

It will be another year before our speaking schedule lightens much, but in the meantime, in the last few months in between meetings we've—

Walked in Kansas cornfields.

Watched trucks unload at a shipping dock.

Played pencil-and-paper "battleship" in a hotel lobby.

Watched pizza dough being tossed.

Gawked, from the outside, at Harry Truman's boyhood home.

Seen rabbits and goats being judged at a county fair.

Seen dragonflies nesting in a Mississippi bayou.

Wandered through churches, a Mormon temple, old graveyards, shopping malls, a Civil War museum, and a zoo. (When have *you* last wandered through a zoo?)

When we don't have time for any of those things we do this: we close our eyes for five to ten minutes and imagine we're at a favorite vacation spot. We imagine it as vividly as possible, with all the physical sensations that we'd notice if we were actually there: the sights, the sounds, the smells, the feeling of wind in our hair or sun on our skin. . . .

After only a few minutes, our bodies begin to relax and respond as though we were actually there.

Or check this possibility: When you start for the shower, could you take a bath instead? A shower's quicker, but a bath could give you a mini-vacation. Besides, remember what the Japanese say, that no great thoughts are ever born in a shower!

Learn to take thousands of tiny vacations—just enough to get you refreshed for that next meeting, that next task—to maintain staying power for your work. Keep refueling midflight.

You say you want another idea? Well, keep a joke book nearby. Chuckle your way to a little momentary relaxation whenever you need it.

For instance, if you're feeling tight right now, do you know what Jesus said at the Last Supper that didn't get put into the Bible?

He said, "Fellas, you'll all have to move to this side of the table, if you want to get in the picture."

If life hands you
a bunch of
lemons,
make
lemon chiffon pie

C H A P T E R 11

What Makes People Shipwreck Their Faith

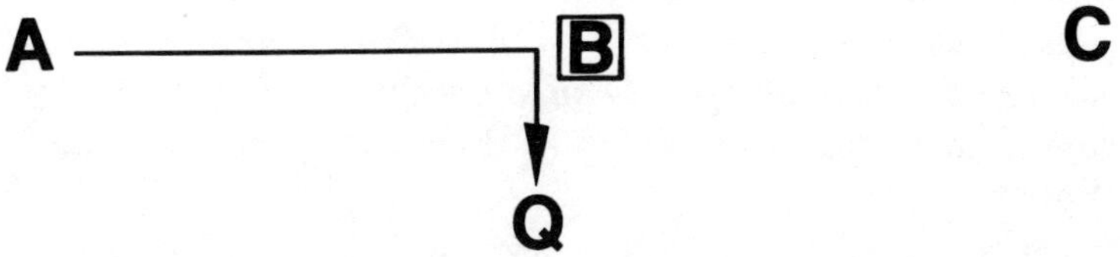

"I fear," wrote the Apostle Paul, "that after enlisting others for the race, I myself might be declared unfit and ordered to stand aside" (1 Cor. 9:27 TLB).

The fear of being disqualified, of being weeded out, is a healthy fear. In fact, it's essential for you, if you're going to persevere—stay lean, disciplined, and "going for the gold."

The prize is at the end. And meanwhile, along the marathon of life, you see bodies drop almost every day. How about you: will you survive to receive your reward?

When we first went to minister at the Lake Avenue Congregational Church in Pasadena, Dr. James Henry Hutchins was just retiring after pastoring there for thirty-eight years. He'd been the minister of that church for almost three years before the two of us were even born! (When we resigned twenty years later, it meant that Lake Avenue had had only two senior pastors in over fifty-eight years.)

Close to seventy, erect and dignified, Dr. Hutchins was the object of our respect for many reasons, but even for just plain *surviving*. We used to say to each other, "It's not hard to honor him. To have ministered all those years without scandal, without major battles, with one wife, with long-term friends—he's got to be a good man."

Why do people drop out along the road? What makes the bodies fall? Why are godly young people so numerous and godly older ones so rare? The Scriptures seem to list at least four reasons why the ranks get thinned.

1. *They loosen their grip on their faith and on the precious possession of a good conscience.* First Timothy 1:19 says that people who let go of these "have shipwrecked their faith."

Defection can be a subtle, gradual thing. Little compromising choices are made. . . .

Maybe right then there's not a strong influence in their lives; maybe they're irregular at attending church; they're not seeing their godly friends. . . .

They're not reading the Bible, so their thinking isn't God's thinking, and their own rationalizations begin to substitute:

"I just don't have to take all this."

"So-and-so did what I'm considering, and his life is turning out great."

"This is ruining my health."

"After all, why can't I try for a little happiness? It's the only life I've got."

"Those affected won't mind too much; they're pretty mature."

"If my friends can't stick this out with me, what kind of friends are they, anyway? Who needs them?"

When rationalizing substitutes for God's thinking, unbelievable words lodge in their minds and come out of their mouths. Recently we've heard not one, but two,

Christian men who've walked out on their wives for other women say, "I can worship God better now; I've never been happier; praise the Lord!" Such Scriptures as Matthew 5:32 or 1 Corinthians 6:18–20 are the farthest things from their minds. We shudder to think of God's assessment:

> These people come near to me with their mouth
> and honor me with their lips,
> but their hearts are far from me (Isa. 29:13).

The consequences will be awesome.

And the two of us frequently say, "We could shipwreck, too! Everybody's just one step away from disaster." Like you, we've got to remain scared to death of becoming "throwaways"—and all our lives hold fast to our faith and our good consciences.

And people shipwreck, says the Bible, because—

2. *They're overtaken by a desire to get rich:*

> People who want to get rich fall into temptation and a trap and into many foolish and harmful desires that plunge men into ruin and destruction (1 Tim. 6:9).

Sounds as if we have to choose between money and God. Not at all!

It's like dog training. When food arrives on the scene, a bad-mannered dog will lunge and tear at it and grab all he can get. With training he learns to control himself and wait patiently until his master gives it to him—and gives him the amount that the dog's best health requires.

A Christian who doesn't trust God to feed him will grab for all he can get—not understanding that God says that "godliness with contentment is *great gain*" (1 Tim. 6:6, emphasis added)! God will feed you well, if you let Him feed you on His terms, while you give yourself to worthier concerns.

You've seen what we've seen: young people in their twenties and thirties, in the A Zone of their careers, who are so wild for money that they shipwreck themselves on the rocks of tensions, adultery, overdrinking, instability, fights, bankruptcies, and in general "the crazies." Their little ones pay a terrible price, and so do they.

For the love of money is a root of all kinds of evil. Some people, eager for money, have wandered from the faith and pierced themselves with many griefs (1 Tim. 6:10).

And people shipwreck, says God's Word, because—

3. *They pride themselves on theological and philosophical knowledge!* You mean to say it isn't good to know a lot?

Of course it is. Paul prayed that we would be "filled with the knowledge of [God's] will through all spiritual wisdom and understanding" (Col. 1:9).

And where is that knowledge to be found? Wrote Paul, "Know the mystery of God, namely, Christ" (Col. 2:1–2).

Knowledge centered on Him is life.

Knowledge centered on ourselves is self-destructing:

Turn away from the godless chatter and the opposing ideas of what is falsely called knowledge, which some have professed and in so doing have wandered from the faith (1 Tim. 6:20–21).

Do you pride yourself in doctrinal understanding? And are you a natural debater? Then be careful. Have a fear of shipwreck! Be occupied not with doctrines about Christ, but with Christ Himself.

And here's a fourth reason people shipwreck:

4. *They just don't trust God later on, the way they did when they were new believers.* So says Hebrews 3:12–14.

The ultimate reason for dropping out is just wandering away from Him.

When we were on a radio talk show recently and people were phoning in about their marriage situations, more than one said, "Well, a while back I got away from the Lord, and then I had this affair. . . ."

Writes Chuck Swindoll with great passion,

> I'll tell you, when you choose to walk away from the Lord and thumb your nose at His grace, He sets the hounds of heaven against you. He does not let His children run wayward or play in the streets of the world without exerting a great deal of discipline. . . .
>
> When you're in the divine woodshed and under His discipline, you know it. It's miserable and bitter.[1]

Sometimes people say to us, "But it's *hard* to walk with the Lord!" And we say, "But it's harder not to!" "It is a dreadful thing to fall into the hands of the living God" (Heb. 10:31).

During World War II there was a giant of a Christian who was known all over the West Coast for the fervent, gutsy way he discipled young men. He was a primary reason why we are in the ministry today.

A generation later, when we came back to California to pastor, this same fellow was up the street from our church frying hamburgers in a little joint. He had divorced his wife for somebody else; he never went to church; he was bitter and embarrassed and hassled by a thousand problems. He was a broken man. (We hear he has since finally come back to the Lord.)

During those same World War II years there was a huge West Coast church launching dozens of young men into the Gospel ministry. One of the favorites among these fellows was taller, better looking, and more fun than almost any of them. You would have voted him "most likely to succeed."

Within a few years he was far away from his loved ones, his former standards, and his Savior. When we last

1. *Three Steps Forward, Two Steps Back* (Nashville: Thomas Nelson, 1980), pp. 170–171.

heard about him, he was a loner driving a cab in New York City.

Ending up in the Q Zone is degrading, humiliating, bitter. It is literally "the pits."

No wonder there's this famous story about Sir Winston Churchill, who near the end of his distinguished career was asked to return to and speak at his old school, Harrow (where as a boy he'd almost flunked out).

The headmaster had been preparing the students to listen to every word because, he said, "In a few days the greatest orator of our time—perhaps of all time—will address you."

The great day finally arrived, and after the school's fanfare and acclamation Sir Winston stood to his feet, acknowledged the introduction, and gave the following address, which is quoted in full:

> Young men, never give up.
> Never give up!
> Never give up!!
> Never, never, never—never—never!

Begin, persevere, win!

"My men are not braver
than other troops—they
are just brave five
minutes longer"

—General Wellington

CHAPTER 12

Three Kinds of Temptations, Four Reasons the Devil Wants You to Yield, and One Powerful Reason Why You Shouldn't

"But," you say, "you don't know the temptations I face."

Yes, we really do. There are only three basic kinds, and the two of us face them all and so does everyone else.

Just as every phase of your living has three time zones—and recognizing them, you'll know what to expect and you'll handle them successfully—so there are three categories of temptations, and every one that comes up you can recognize and say, "Aha! I'm on to you, too, temptation! And I still say no."

> For all that is in the world—the lust of the flesh, the lust of the eyes, and the pride of life—is not of the Father but is of the world (1 John 2:16 NKJV).

"The lust of the flesh, the lust of the eyes, and the pride of life"—every temptation you'll ever have crops up in one or several of these three forms.

There was Eve, looking at the fruit of that tree in the Garden:

> When the woman saw that the fruit of the tree was good for food [the lust of the flesh] and pleasing to the eye [the lust of the eyes], and also desirable for gaining wisdom [the pride of life], she took some and ate it (Gen. 3:6).

To her it was a triple whammy, and she succumbed.

To be tempted is not wrong. Don't feel guilty when you're tempted! Eve did not sin until she yielded. Someone has said, "You can't stop a bird from landing on your head, but you can keep him from building a nest in your hair."

The Lord Jesus was "tempted in every way, just as we are—yet without sin" (Heb. 4:15). We can say that Jesus lived *through* life. Most of us live a portion of life, but Jesus experienced it *all* for us. Luke says He "finished every temptation" (Luke 4:13).

Three punishing attacks of Satan upon Jesus are displayed for us to see. They summarize temptations we all face:

1. *"Tell these stones to become bread"* (Matt. 4:3). In Jesus' time of greatest hunger, Satan appealed to the lust of the flesh.

The Lord was soon to feed others miraculously; it wasn't that He couldn't follow Satan's suggestion. The temptation here was not to wait for God the Father to provide His food, but to act independently of the Father when He was hungry and to provide for Himself.

You will be tempted to fulfill your desires on your terms: "I want what I want when I want it!" You can ask for the right thing at the wrong time. (That's certainly true of sex; it's a good gift from God, but at the right God-given time—in the marriage relationship.)

2. *"If You are the Son of God, throw Yourself down"* from the highest point of the temple (Matt. 4:6), appealing to the pride of life. His purpose? To get Jesus to go on an "ego trip." Let Him dive off the high temple and come swooping down like Superman.

But Jesus refused cheap heroics to get attention. He could wait for the glory that God would give, and not seek to drum up His own.

3. *"Bow down and worship me,"* said Satan, taking

Jesus to a very high mountain and showing Him all the kingdoms of the world and their splendor, appealing to the lust of the eye. "All this I will give you if you will bow down and worship me" (Matt. 4:8–9).

And with this enticement the devil promised that he would make Christ a world power without the cross and all that suffering. He passed before Jesus' vision the world and all its glory, beauty, and strength—all its art, thought, and work. "Worship me, and all you see will be yours," said Satan.

But Jesus wasn't after earthly kingdoms; He was after *the* Kingdom. There could never be His ultimate crown without the cross. He kept His eye on that future C Zone! He knew what you and we must always remember: the temporary is no substitute for the eternal. And so "for the joy that was set before Him," He endured and resisted temptation.

Friend, so can you!

Satan will come after you in the fiercest temptations. He'll attack you in your three areas of weakness:

1. *The lust or the cravings of the flesh:* sexual immorality, overeating, addictive habits, laziness. . . .

2. *The lust or the cravings of your eyes:* excessive desires for beauty of any kind—cars, interior decorating, clothes, other persons of the opposite sex. . . .

3. *The pride of life:* overgrown appetites for money, status, or power, which lead to jealousy, slander, cheating, and "every form of malice" (Eph. 4:31).

Why won't Satan leave you alone? Because *he hates you for at least four reasons.*

One is that God loves you, and whatever is loved by God is hated by the devil.

Another is that the Christian, being a child of God, bears a family resemblance to the Father and to the household of faith. When Satan sees you, he thinks of Him!

A third reason is that a true Christian is a former slave who has escaped from the galley, and Satan cannot forgive him for this affront.

A fourth reason is this, as A. W. Tozer puts it:

> A praying Christian is a constant threat to the stability of Satan's government. The Christian is a holy rebel loose in the world with access to the throne of God. Satan never knows from what direction the danger will come. Who knows when another Elijah will arise, or another Daniel? or a Luther or a Booth? Who knows when an Edwards or a Finney may go in and liberate a whole town or countryside by the preaching of the Word and prayer? Such a danger is too great to tolerate, so Satan gets to the new convert as early as possible to prevent his becoming too formidable a foe.[1]

There you are: you're a sitting duck for the enemy's attacks.

But we want you to see a powerful reason why you shouldn't yield to him.

Mentally climb that tree again and get another panoramic view—this time not just of your own life but of the lives of generations before you and after you. Think big. Stretch your horizons.

As God looks down on the total human scene, He sees each individual, of course. (Aren't the genealogies in the Bible a comfort for that reason?)

But He does more. He also sees the whole human scene; He sees the connection, the mergings together, the patterns and the oneness of the generations that even from our treetop we can barely envision. Without the limits of time, looking down over all at once, God sees how you belong to your great-grandfather and how you affect your great-grandson and how in every par-

1. "The Editorial Voice," *The Alliance Weekly* magazine, March 6, 1963.

ticular detail you are part of the continuum of the human generations.

Who but God could think of this kind of logic?—He says that Melchizedek was even greater than the great high priest Levi, who lived three generations later—as proved by the fact that Levi, in the body of his great-grandfather Abraham, bowed down to Melchizedek and paid him tithes (see Heb. 7:9–10)!

Mysterious! Awesome!

What did *you* do in the body of your great-grandfather? And what are you doing today which is an action of your child, your grandchild, or your great-grandchild?

God gives hints of a commingling together of the behavior of generations which is unthinkable to us little people with limited perception. First Peter 1:12 says that God revealed to the prophets of old that when they wrote, they were not serving themselves but you! Centuries ago they thought about you. They wrote for you.

You and we are holding hands with a great host of unseen persons in unbroken chains.

What happens when you freak out and say, "Oh, heck, I quit"?

When you kick over the traces?

When you flee, when you say "I've had it," when you give up?

What damage is that doing to the others—the whole chain of your ancestors and your descendants? What kind of permanent wound or scar are you making? What instability are you building into the line? How many will grieve? How many will be hurt?

Maybe at that Great Day we'll see larger reasons to weep over sins than we ever dreamed—or more glorious reasons to rejoice over temptations resisted and victories won!

Ask God for staying power, for determination, for patience, for gutsy courage to survive and survive well.

Everyone faces temptations. How will you handle yours? Will you blame others and crumple, or will you come out a winner?

Your fortitude could have larger ramifications than you now know.

Begin, persevere, win!

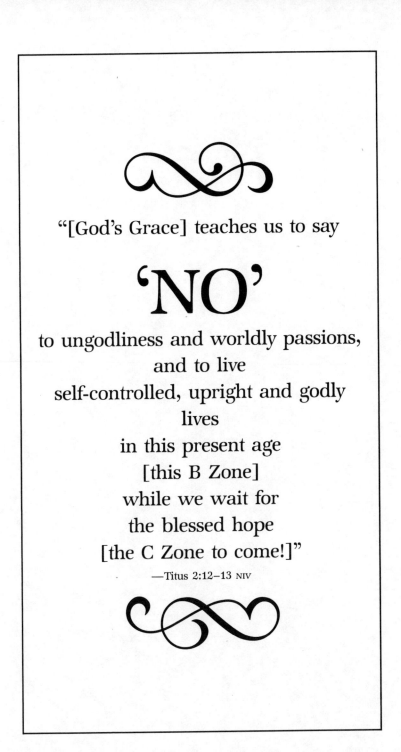

“[God’s Grace] teaches us to say

‘NO’

to ungodliness and worldly passions,
and to live
self-controlled, upright and godly
lives
in this present age
[this B Zone]
while we wait for
the blessed hope
[the C Zone to come!]”

—Titus 2:12–13 NIV

CHAPTER 13

Take Advantage of God's Rehabilitation Program

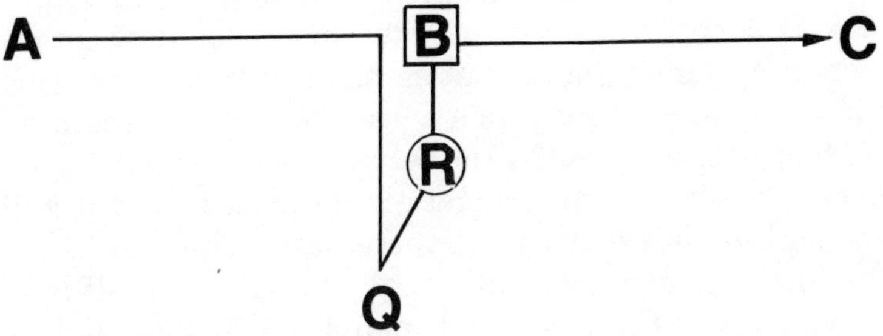

It was New Year's Day in the 1930 Rose Bowl. Roy Reigels of USC picked up a Georgia Tech fumble, but he got excited and began racing down the field in the wrong direction, toward his own goal line.

One of his own teammates finally tackled him and brought him down, but Tech took the ball and scored right before halftime.

In the locker room Roy Reigels cried like a baby.

Coach Price announced, "The same men who played first half will start the second."

The team started out to the field, all but Roy.

"Coach," he said, "I can't do it! I've ruined you, I've ruined SC. I can't face that crowd!"

Mr. Price touched his shoulder. "Roy," he said, "go on out. The game's not over yet."

Reigels went back into the game, and Tech players

said they never saw anyone play football as Roy Reigels played in the second half of the 1930 Rose Bowl game.

And you have failed in the past, and so have we. Do you feel disqualified? Do you feel as if you're already a "throwaway," that you "blew it" and you can't undo your mistakes? Does your record seem too blotted? Were your injuries too damaging, your mistakes too irreversible?

Friend, *your problem is no longer those past sins; your problem is how you're presently handling those sins.*

You have two choices.

1. You may choose chronic regret that leaves you in the Q Zone for the rest of your life. It could be an attempt at a do-it-yourself atonement; if you believe God doesn't easily forgive, then a way you can do something to help the process is by the penance of perpetual regret. That's a terrible misunderstanding of God. And it will do nothing but leave you unnecessarily shipwrecked.

That kind of regret can actually be a form of self-love. A person can think so highly of himself that any failure to live up to his own image of himself deeply disappoints him. He feels he's "betrayed his better self"—that even if God forgives him, he can't forgive himself. So he joins all the other hurt, angry, egocentric Q Zoners in their everlasting "pity party."

2. Or you can choose "godly sorrow" over those past sins:

> Godly sorrow brings repentance that leads to salvation and leaves no regret (2 Cor. 7:10).

The father of the prodigal son put on a big party to honor his return. Now, the son wouldn't have made his father happier by sitting in a corner during the party mourning over his past. He honored his father by taking his word for it that all was really forgiven.

Regret over the sins of the past will haunt you until you truly believe how thoroughly God blots out your sins.

Blessed is he
  whose transgressions are forgiven,
  whose sins are covered.
Blessed is the man
  whose sin the LORD does not count against him
  and in whose spirit is no deceit (Ps. 32:1–2).

Nobody's life is a smooth A-through-B-through-C-Zone with every problem courageously tackled and cleanly defeated. A paraphrase of Romans 3:23 could be that 100 percent of us have messed up things we began, and sometimes we didn't persevere and we *didn't* win, we fell into Q Zones.

If sin kept people from getting to C Zones, no one would ever get there, because all have sinned. But God has already taken care of that; Christ died for that! That problem is already conquered. Believe how defeated sin really is, and don't try to use a dead enemy as an excuse for not winning the battle!

No one can undo past wrongs; no one can atone for a single sin; so we all start out at the same place: forgiven in Christ, with our past record accounted as clean. We're saved by His grace, and we live by that same grace.

Listen, as long as God continues to give you life, He has at least one glorious C Zone ahead for you. Then, as the two of us told the young missionary women, don't quit before you quit! Don't die before you die! If you check out emotionally and mentally ahead of time, you've aborted; you've truly quit; and your remaining life will be filled with negative memories, wounds, scars, and self-doubts, and you'll just be "grinding it out till the time's up."

Is that what you want?

"But," you say, "I checked out so long ago. I've had so many wasted years in the Q Zone! Surely it's too late for me."

Jesus in John 5 healed a man who'd been paralyzed for thirty-eight years. Peter in Acts 3 and 4 healed a man crippled from birth who was past forty. Why should God be stymied by a time factor?

King Manasseh had years of messing up his reign over Judah:

> He did evil in the sight of the LORD, following the detestable practices of the nations the LORD had driven out before the Israelites. He rebuilt the high places; . . . he also erected altars to the Baals, . . . he bowed down to all the starry hosts and worshiped them (2 Chron. 33:2–3).

Finally God had had enough. He arranged it so that the Babylonians captured Manasseh, "put a hook in his nose, bound him with bronze shackles and took him to Babylon" (2 Chron. 33:11–22). Ouch! Pain and humiliation!

And here's an interesting thing. Finally, when God had had enough, Manasseh had also had enough:

> In his distress he sought the favor of the LORD his God and humbled himself greatly before the God of his fathers (2 Chron. 33:12).

We might have said, "Sorry, Manasseh, but I can't forget all the damage you did in the past. You blew it, and you're now getting what you deserve."

But God is not like us!

> And when [Manasseh] prayed to him, the Lord was moved by his entreaty and listened to his plea; so he brought him back to Jerusalem and to his kingdom. Then Manasseh knew that the LORD is God (2 Chron. 33:13).

Now God lifted him out of his Q Zone and into the place of His tender rehabilitation. And Manasseh didn't say a word about his "luck turning"; Manasseh knew it was God.

The last years of his reign were like the second half of Roy Reigels's 1930 Rose Bowl game. He became some kind of motivated tiger!

He rebuilt the outer wall of the City of David . . . he also made it much higher. He stationed military commanders in all the fortified cities in Judah. He got rid of the foreign gods and removed the image from the temple of the LORD, as well as all the altars he had built on the temple hill and in Jerusalem; and he threw them out of the city. Then he restored the altar of the LORD and sacrificed fellowship and thank offerings on it, and told Judah to serve the LORD, the God of Israel (2 Chron. 33:14–16).

Have you any idea the glorious life that could be yet ahead for you, if you take advantage of God's rehabilitation program?

If regrets over the past have kept you from moving forward, understand that those very regrets need God's forgiveness, too. The negative memories, the wounds, the scars, the self-doubts—bring them all to the feet of Jesus and confess them as part of the whole mess of your sin. And—

If we confess our sins, he is faithful and just and will forgive us our sins and purify us from all unrighteousness (1 John 1:9, emphasis added).

So don't cry over your past. For you it's halftime in the locker room, and the coach is saying, "Go on out. The game's not over yet."

Begin again, persevere, and win!

"Success is never
final.
Failure is never
fatal.
It is
courage
that counts"
—Sir Winston Churchill

C H A P T E R 1 4

For Future Success: Staying Power Through Mental Concentration

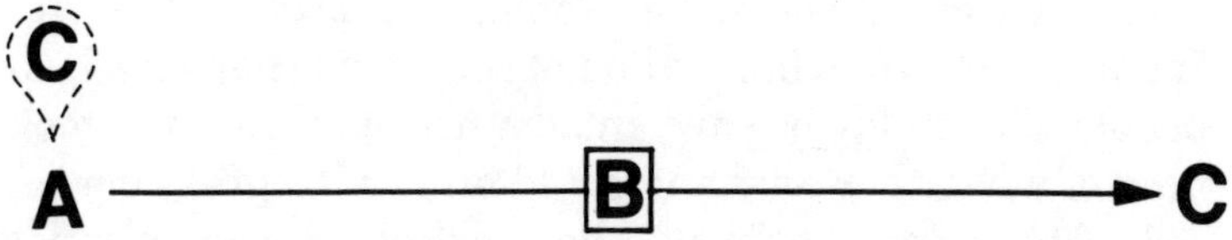

A professional golfer mentally pictures winning shots—and then plays them.

An ambitious hostess visualizes a larger home—and eventually moves in.

A salesman concentrates on envisioning a million dollar sale—and makes it.

You remember we said earlier, *"You are, in truth, being shaped by your future. And the more you believe in that future, keep your eyes on it, and move toward it, the more strongly it will influence and shape you."*

The powers of the mind are fantastic. We've learned in past days to give the mind consistent input under certain conditions to produce hypnotism and brainwashing, but now there's this easier, do-it-yourself trick going around: visualizing goals in advance in order to achieve them.

The trouble is, this power can be used for either good or bad.

The professional golfer can mentally picture winning shots—and make enough money to divorce his wife.

The ambitious hostess can visualize a larger home—and it becomes her spiritual undoing.

The salesman can focus his mind on that million-dollar sale—and drink his way to personal defeat.

So we need to be careful what pictures we continually put in our minds; they may not be what's good for us. Psalm 106:15 says that God gave the Israelites what they insisted on—"but sent leanness into their soul."

On the other hand, Hebrews, chapter 11, seems to say that faith is, in one sense, something pretty close: it's "being certain of what we do not see." And then God lists people who by faith "saw" in advance of reality and took hold of what they saw and acted on it with great power:

1. Abel correctly "saw" the need of a blood sacrifice centuries before it was commonly understood—and uniquely pleased God, verse 4.

2. Noah correctly "saw" a coming flood—and saved himself and his family, verse 7.

3. Abraham "was looking forward" in advance to a land he would later receive as an inheritance—and he traveled "blindly" to it and settled down, verses 8–10. Then he strongly believed a future for himself and Sarah as parents, though they were past age, and he became the father of multitudes, verses 11–12.

4. Isaac correctly envisioned glorious futures for his sons—and blessed them with prophetic words, verse 20.

5. Jacob did the same, verse 21.

6. Joseph pictured, four hundred years ahead of time, the escape of his brother Jews from Egypt—and gave instructions about his bones, verse 22.

7. Moses' parents correctly believed a future for their threatened baby—and saved his life, verse 23.

8. Moses "was looking ahead to [his] reward" and correctly "saw" coming glory for himself and his enslaved

Jewish brothers. So he aligned himself with them rather than with Pharaoh's court, verses 24–27—and he "persevered because he saw him who is invisible," thus becoming one of the greatest leaders of all time.

9. A whole army of Israel accurately envisioned the collapse of an enemy city in seven days, verse 30.

Verses 13–16 of Hebrews 11 explain *what these people did to see the future with telescopic vision:*

The Greek verb, *aspazomai,* in verse 13 means "embraced," "sought," "desired," "wanted," "reached for," "looked for," "welcomed."

In verse 14, *epizēteō,* it's "was eager for," "desired earnestly," "looked for."

In verse 16, *oregō*, it's "were longing for," "were thinking of," "were remembering," "were making mention of."

On the other hand,

> If they had been thinking of the country they had left, they would have had opportunity to return (v. 15).

But they weren't focusing on their A Zone, the "good old days." Looking backward begins within people a process of dying.

And they weren't concentrating solely on their B Zone, with no sense of future direction.

(Alice in Wonderland came to a fork in the road and didn't know which way to turn. She looked up and there was a grinning Cheshire Cat.

"Please, Mr. Cat, help me. Tell me which road I should take."

"That depends," said the cat. "Where are you going?"

"I don't know," muttered the confused Alice.

"Then it doesn't matter," said the cat.)

No, these Old Testament people were strongly picturing specific futures, dwelling on them in their minds and earnestly desiring them—which kindled within them life and hope, courage and optimism and staying power.

The vast difference between humanistic visualizing and the picturing by faith described here is that their egos didn't dream up these things—*God told them what was coming.*

Now, look at this carefully, for your own life.

Verse 1 defines faith in this way:

> Faith is being sure of what we hope for and certain of what we do not see.

And verse 6 says, "And without faith [without strongly "seeing" what we cannot see] it is impossible to please God, because anyone who comes to him must believe that he exists and that he rewards those who earnestly seek him."

Remarkably, God insists that you—

1. Believe that He is true;
2. Believe that all His coming rewards for you are true;
3. Move forward by faith and live in the reality of them.

Believing in and picturing your coming C Zone will give you staying power.

> So do not throw away your confidence [says Heb. 10:35ff.], it will be richly rewarded.

You need to persevere so that when you have done the will of God, you will receive what he has promised:

> *For in just a very little while,*
> *He who is coming will come and will not delay.*
> *But my righteous one* [*that is, righteous because he believes*] *will live by faith.*
> *And if he shrinks back,*
> *I will not be pleased with him.*

So here's the sequence:

A ZONE	B ZONE	C ZONE
CRISIS →	***PROCESS FOR STAYING POWER*** →	***CONCLUSION***
Believing that God is, and that he rewards those who seek him (Heb. 11:6).	Not "shrinking back" but by deliberate habit, through good times and hard times, still strongly believing in His reality and His rewards.	Seeing God face to face (1 John 3:2,3) and receiving our full rewards,

Do you get the picture?

So we fix our eyes not on what is seen, but on what is unseen. For what is seen is temporary, but what is unseen is eternal (2 Cor. 4:18).

We "fix our eyes"! That's visualizing. Picture God's desired goals for you in advance (better than any you could have dreamed up for yourself), and picture them regularly and frequently until they come true. It will keep you steady. It will give you staying power, for life.

Get to know where God wants to take you.

Jim Hefley, ex-editor, ex-pastor, professional writer, decided at age forty-nine to work to get a Ph.D. in mass communications:

The first weeks were the hardest. . . . Cold mornings spent trying to find a parking place, then rushing to class. Awkward exchanges with fellow students the age of my children. Long tiresome drives back home. Late night toiling over tedious research papers. Many times I wondered, "Why am I punishing myself?"

Now, the next sentence is the answer:

After each questioning, assurance would come . . . that the sacrifice was worth what the graduate degree would mean for the rest of my life.[1]

For Jim Hefley, a mental picture of his goal told him *what* to do and kept him doing it.

For the great French impressionistic painter Renoir, a mental picture of his goal told him *what not* to do:

Renoir at one point suffered total paralysis in his legs. For two years a doctor worked on them to bring their life back and help Renoir walk again.

At last the doctor succeeded. With great effort the famous painter stood and actually walked across the room. Then painfully, he made his way back to his invalid chair and surrendered to it, for life. "I give up," he said. "It takes all my will power, and I would have nothing left for painting."

Renoir's biographer, his own son Jean, says that after the immutable decision not to walk, Renoir's paintings for the rest of his life were "a display of fireworks to the end, . . . freed from all theories, from all fears."[2]

Let God give you a view, a vision, of your future. Only at that point will you know what to do and what not to do—how to "eliminate and concentrate"! Wrote Andrew Murray,

And now, who is ready to enter into this New and everlasting Covenant with his whole heart? Let each of us do it.

Begin by asking God very humbly to give you, by the Spirit who dwells in you, the vision of the heavenly life of whole-hearted love and obedience, as it has actually been prepared

1. James C. Hefley, *Life Changes* (Wheaton, Ill.: Tyndale, 1984), pp. 40–41.

2. Quoted in the *Los Angeles Times,* March 16, 1985.

for you in Christ. It is an existing reality, a spiritual endowment out of the life of God which can come upon you. . . .

Ask earnestly, definitely, believingly, that God can reveal this to you. Rest not till you know fully what your Father means you to be, and has provided for your most certainly being.

When you begin to see [it], . . . offer yourself to God unreservedly to be taken up into it.[3]

For your life, look beyond, beyond . . .
And picture it as clearly as you can . . .
Until faith becomes literal sight.
Begin, . . .
Persevere, . . .
Win!

3. Andrew Murray, *The Two Covenants* (Old Tappan, N.J.: Fleming H. Revell, 1974), pp. 165–166.

If your
ole truck's
gonna make it
over the hills,
get your speed up
when you're
in the valley

C H A P T E R 1 5

For Future Success: Staying Power Through Disciplines

Do you know how you sculpt an elephant? It's easy: you just get a large rock and cut away everything that doesn't look like an elephant.

Don't laugh, there's a great truth here. You may look at your life with all its activities and interests, some important and some clutter, and it looks to you like a huge, unwieldy mass—a big rock—with little potential for getting through your B Zone to a life that wins.

But when you have "visualized," when you have pictured mentally what God is calling you to be and therefore what *you* want to be, then you can methodically start cutting away everything that doesn't contribute to that.

That's your need: a dream for your life, the vision that God will give you. And when you begin to see its shape, you'll think, *Well, certainly* this *activity isn't compatible, and probably* that *ought to go. . . .*

And you'll say, *If I'm going to be this in my C Zone, then I need to prepare myself these days by this, this, and this.* Eliminate and concentrate! Live your present life building toward your wonderful future!

A little girl was looking at Michelangelo's statue of David, and she said in wonder to the great sculptor, "How did you know he was in there?"

People who learn to visualize see Davids in rocks.

Michelangelo needed a mental picture of David before he knew what to cut away.

And the more is cut away, the more important is what remains! The rock that's left is becoming a David!—or maybe at least an elephant!

What we're trying to say is this: when you've pared away superfluous areas from your life (and only you and God will know what they are), the remaining activities must be right. Your life will be increasingly precious, and how you spend it, increasingly important. Isn't that exciting and wonderful?

> Only one life—
> 'Twill soon be past.
> Only what's done
> For Christ will last.

Someone is saying, "You're getting legalistic. My salvation isn't based on works; it's based on faith."

And we answer, we're not talking about salvation. We're assuming you're already a Christian, and we're saying with Peter, "Make every effort to add to your faith goodness, . . . knowledge, . . . self-control, . . . perseverance, . . . godliness, . . . brotherly kindness, and . . . love" (2 Pet. 1:5–7). "Add to your faith": supplement it, flesh it out. Being a Christian doesn't mean believing and then just sitting around. Now that you have faith in God's part, make every effort—that's your part.

That's disciplines.

That's regular "holy habits."

That's pacing yourself for the cross-country run to the C Zone.

Says Henri Nouwen, "A spiritual life without discipline is impossible." Tighten your belt. Get tough on yourself. GOFORIT.

A woman once said to the great Paderewski, "Sir, you are truly a genius."

"Well," he answered, "before I was a genius, I was a drudge!"

To get there, to win—your life needs discipline, order, and arrangement.

Make out your coming week's schedule, and mark in your disciplines first—the top priority things that you must *do,* in your B Zone, to *become,* in your C Zone.

Live your life, not doing things from moment to moment because you feel like it, but doing things decided on in advance, because it's the time you set to do them.

Be in control! Manage your life; don't let it manage you—blown here and there by every little wind that comes along.

Employ the principle of firsts:

"I have only so much time every day. I believe the Bible is more important than the newspaper; therefore I will read the Bible *first.*"

"I believe helping my neighbor is more important than this crossword puzzle; therefore I will help my neighbor *first.*"

Lace needs holes as well as thread. But build your life into a planned pattern of thread first, and the holes will take care of themselves.

Music needs rests as well as notes. But build your life into a planned rhythm of notes first, and the rests will fall naturally into their places.

When you become steady in your "holy habits," your emotions will become steady, your disposition will become steady, your optimism and courage will be steady: you'll be a steady person.

If your "disciplines" are off-again, on-again, so will your life be—so will *you* be. And how will the pattern of your lace look? How will the rhythm of your music sound?

Make your life beautiful with planned, regular disciplines.

Mr. Paderewski also said once, "If I don't practice for one day, I can tell it. If I don't practice for two days, my friends can tell it. And if I don't practice for three days, the public can tell it."

What are possible disciplines for your life?

1. *Prayer.* A minister was asked once to offer a prayer before the New York state legislature. Everybody was shocked when he rose to his feet and said, "I will not pray for you. There are certain things a man must do for himself. He must blow his own nose, make his own love, and say his own prayers"!!

We agree with you, that was a little rude. But the fact is, nobody can do your praying for you by proxy. It is totally up to you: either you establish a life of prayer, or you don't.

"O my God," wrote Madame Guyon, "if the value of prayer were but known . . . Let the poor come, let the ignorant and carnal come; let the children without reason or knowledge come, let the dull or hard hearts which can retain nothing come to the practice of prayer, and they shall become wise."[1]

"Oh, the value of prayer . . . !" It is so key, it may make the difference between your having staying power through to the C Zone or your dropping into the Q Zone.

"But I pray!" say "mini-Christians." "I pray when I drive the car, and I pray when I jog. . . ."

If we learn anything about prayer in Scripture, we learn that it is not only instantaneous during activity, but perhaps even more, it's withdrawing from everything else to give Him our full attention.

We mutter and sputter.
We fume and we spurt.

1. Madame Guyon, *Madame Guyon* (Chicago: Moody Press), pp. 40, 41.

We mumble and grumble.
Our feelings get hurt.
We can't understand things.
Our vision grows dim,
When all that we need is
A moment with Him.[2]

"A moment"—well, that's a start. Better a moment every day than longer times sporadically. Did you know that studies show that only that which is done daily is truly revolutionary in our lives?—that only activities done daily make basic, deep grooves in our thinking and personalities?

Let your prayer life, then, become daily.

A. *Have a time.* If your life is regular, make it the same time every day. If your life is irregular like ours, mark your calendar for a week in advance, when it will be, each day.

B. *Have a place.* We have a special chair at home, another at the office. Sometimes each of us seeks the aloneness of our cars, overlooking a park or someplace quiet.

C. *Have an attitude of expectancy.* He wants to meet with you. He longs to talk to you as you talk with Him. As well as speak, listen.

D. *Have a spirit of quiet.* He says to you in Psalm 46:10, "Be still, and know that I am God."

E. *Have a plan.* Why not form your prayer on the acrostic "ACTS"?—

A: Adoration ("Lord, You're wonderful. This is how I picture You. . . .")

C: Confession ("Father, forgive me for. . . .")

T: Thanksgiving ("Thank You for. . . .")

2. Earl D. Radmacher, *You and Your Thoughts* (Palm Springs, Calif.: Ronald N. Haynes, 1982), p. 99.

s: Supplication ("And here are my requests, according to Your will. . . .")[3]

Prayer is to become the foundation, the life, the source, the breath, the atmosphere, of your walk with God.

> The key to true piety is not to subscribe to the ethical teachings of Moses or of Jesus, nor is it to have the right precepts of God and reality. Instead it is being united with Christ by faith, then living the kind of life that proceeds from that union.[4]

Oh, our friend! Get to know God in leisurely prayer! Brother Lawrence wrote about prayer, "If I dare use the expression, I should choose to call this state the bosom of God, for the inexpressible sweetness which I taste and experience there."

2. *Bible study.* A young potential Bible scholar once wrote God a letter which said, "Dear God, I've been reading Your book. I like what You say. Where do You get Your ideas?"

The Bible springs from God Himself, and He is His own source of ideas! That's why there's never been another book like it. It is His "word" to you, His means of communicating with you, His love letter to you.[5]

The more you immerse yourself in it, the better you will know Him.

And the Bible was written to give you staying power!

> For everything that was written in the past was written to teach us, so that through endurance and the encouragement of the Scriptures we might have hope (Rom. 15:4).

3. See Anne Ortlund, *Joanna: A Story of Renewal* (Waco, Tex.: Word, 1986).

4. Donald G. Bloesch, *Faith and Its Counterfeits* (Downers Grove, Ill.: InterVarsity Press, 1981), p. 19.

5. See Raymond C. Ortlund, *Be A New Christian All Your Life* (Old Tappan, N.J.: Fleming H. Revell, 1983), pp. 137–151.

The two of us have been studying the Bible since we were children, but we've been reading it through annually for about the last fifteen years, and every year it grows more exciting, even more novel and surprising!

The Bible speaks for itself, about itself:

And the words of the LORD are flawless,
like silver refined in a furnace of clay,
purified seven times (Ps. 12:6).

Your word is a lamp to my feet
and a light to my path (Ps. 119:105).

I have hidden your word in my heart
that I might not sin against you (Ps. 119:11).

Man does not live on bread alone, but on every word that comes from the mouth of God (Matt. 4:4).

All Scripture is God-breathed and is useful for teaching, rebuking, correcting and training in righteousness, so that the man of God may be thoroughly equipped for every good work (2 Tim. 3:16–7).

And because those things are all true, God tells us, "Let the word of Christ dwell in you richly as you teach and admonish one another with all wisdom" (Col. 3:16).

It's a big book. You won't digest it all overnight. How can it "dwell in you richly"?

Take a piece of it every day. Read enough to get blessed; whether you read two verses or two books, don't quit until it "grabs" you!

Ask two questions as you read, and have notebook and pen ready for your answers. They're the same two questions Saul asked on the road to Damascus:

A. "Who are You, Lord?" (Acts 22:8) and—

B. "What shall I do, Lord?" (Acts 22:10).

In other words, seek to understand all you can about the Lord from the passage you read, and then ask what you should do to apply the Word, to obey it, in the immediate future.

As long as Scripture reading is a merely intellectual exercise, it won't get "deep into your bones." But if you will *obey* it, you'll discover you're truly getting to know both it and its Author, and it will begin to "dwell in you richly."

Then give it out, pass it on! Learn the discipline of capturing—by taking notes—all that you learn and filing it so you can use it again.[6]

Remember the parable about the seed? The good seed of the Word of God fell on four kinds of soil, and in three kinds it had no staying power so that the seed didn't produce.

> But the seed on good soil stands for those with a noble and good heart, who hear the word, retain it, and by persevering produce a crop (Luke 8:15).

That's the discipline of the Word of God in your life:

A. *Hear it,* read it, learn it.

B. *Retain it.* Take notes and file them so that you've permanently captured what you're learning.

C. *And by persevering* . . . ask God for opportunities to pass it on to friends, or teach it in a Sunday school class or Bible class. Be lovingly aggressive!

D. *Produce a crop.* Reproduce yourself in other believers who come to know what you know.[7]

3. *Solitude.* This discipline is different from your quiet time, but one that will greatly help it.

It's not that as soon as we get alone with God, we are

6. See Anne Ortlund, *Disciplines of the Beautiful Woman* (Waco, Tex.: Word, 1977), pp. 82–94, 105, 106.

7. See Anne Ortlund, *Discipling One Another* (Waco, Tex.: Word, 1979).

prepared to hear Him speak. A slot of time is not all that we need. Says Henri Nouwen,

> We are usually surrounded by so much inner and outer noise that it is hard to truly hear our God when he is speaking to us. We have often become deaf. . . . Thus our lives become *absurd*. In the word *absurd* we find the Latin word *surdus,* which means "deaf.". . .
>
> A spiritual discipline is necessary in order to move slowly from an absurd to an obedient life, from a life filled with noisy worries to a life in which there is some free inner space. . . .[8]

Our friend Dr. John Huffman, a very busy pastor, recently described to us with enthusiasm a whole week he had had alone, in a place where he knew no one and almost never spoke. He played golf, he slept, he read, he prayed, he opened up his inner life to the silence for which he was hungry.

You may not have the luxury of that kind of time, but your soul desperately needs aloneness and silence. (A person who's always available isn't worth much when he *is* available.)

Maybe at first you won't be able to stand more than five to ten minutes a day, but make sure it is absolutely *daily.* Be totally alone. Have the television and radio off, take the phone off its hook, close doors if the traffic blares outside, make your atmosphere as quiet and undistracting as possible. Read no books. Do nothing "useful."

When you've gotten rid of your outer distractions, you may become very aware of your inner distractions—the anxieties, the bad memories, the angers, the chaos of your heart. Maybe for a few weeks your solitude will not only seem a waste, but even painful.

But persevere with this discipline! Be deliberately

8. Henri J. M. Nouwen, *Making All Things New* (New York: Harper & Row, 1981), pp. 67–68.

quiet. As neither outer nor inner distractions are fed and attended to, they will gradually withdraw. But you won't become empty, you'll become aware of God and eternity and your stripped-down, quieted, unfolding self.

> The more we train ourselves to spend time with God and him alone, the more we discover that God is with us at all times and in all places. . . .
>
> Once the solitude of time and space has become a solitude of the heart, we will never have to leave that solitude. We will be able to live the spiritual life in any place and any time. Thus the discipline of solitude enables us to live active lives in the world, while remaining always in the presence of the living God.[9]

There are so many other disciplines: simplicity, fasting, ministering to others, abstinences of various kinds, a weekly Sabbath rest, the discipline of regularly partaking in the Lord's Supper, tithing, the singing of hymns, private confession of sins, early rising. . . .

The important thing to remember is that every discipline is not for every Christian, nor is every discipline to be observed all the time.

Athletes use one set of exercises for a while and then leave those to go on to others. Think of these disciplines as spiritual exercises to keep you balanced and fit, and ask God to direct your disciplined life.

Now let us tell you the bottom-line reason why your life needs the practice of these "holy habits."

Look, here are two donkeys harnessed to opposite ends of a cart, pulling in opposite directions.[10]

9. Ibid., pp. 79–80.

10. Idea from Donald Grey Barnhouse, *Teaching the Word of Truth* (Grand Rapids, Mich.: Eerdmans, 1940), p. 31.

Which way will the cart go? Which donkey is going to win?

If you feed the east donkey and starve the west one, before long that cart's going to move east. And if you feed the west donkey and starve the east one, . . . you're right.

You have a vision of your wonderful C Zone. How will you get there?

Feed your holy habits. Strengthen and toughen and encourage all the parts of your life that will move you toward your C Zone. And starve the other parts!

It's another way of saying that wonderful old truth about disciplines that you've heard someplace before, "Do you know how to sculpt an elephant? It's easy: You just get a large rock and cut away everything that doesn't look like an elephant."

"In order to cultivate
good habits we need

WILL POWER.

In order to rid ourselves
of bad habits, we need

WON'T POWER"

—Moishe Rosen
Director, Jews for Jesus

C H A P T E R 16

Steer Clear of the Shaky and the Flaky

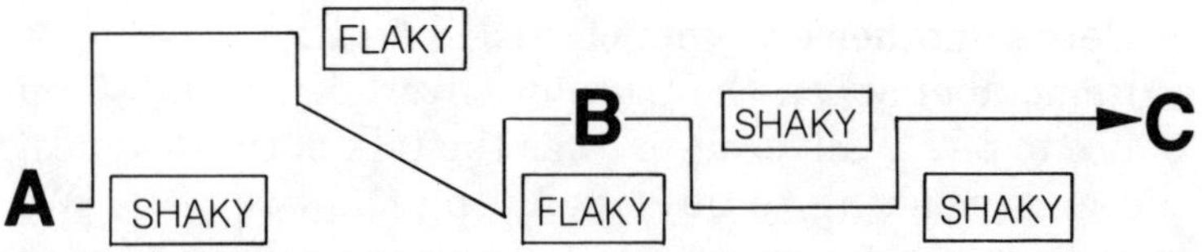

We worked through lots of titles for this chapter. We called it "For Steadiness, Anchor Yourself to What Is Steady"; "Put Your Trust Only in What Has Staying Power"; "Establish Yourself by Trusting Only in What Is Established"; "Put Your Ultimate Trust in What Is Ultimate"; "Hang onto What Is Ultimate"; "Hang onto What Lasts"; "Last By Hanging onto What Lasts. . . ."

Well, you can tell what we wanted to get across—that you do have to be picky about what you rely on.

You see, *faith can be misled.*

Our granddaughter Beth Anne, age six, discovered last Christmas that Santa Claus isn't real. But of course everybody knows that the Tooth Fairy is real; that's one of the solid facts of life.

So Beth Anne felt terrible the other morning when she woke up at five o'clock with her tooth still under her pillow. She went in to her parents complaining, "The Tooth Fairy forgot me!"

"It's too early," said Walt, her dad. "The night isn't

over. Probably the Tooth Fairy is still making his rounds." And with a quarter somehow in his hand, he guided her back to bed, tucked her in, and slipped the quarter under her pillow.

Later when Sherry, her mother, went in to get her up for the day Beth Anne was lying there awake and consoled.

"The Tooth Fairy still forgot me," she said, "but I saw Daddy give me a quarter, anyway."

Now, Beth Anne's faith in the Tooth Fairy has real staying power! Unfortunately, it's misled faith.

Here's another example of misled faith.

Remember when the price of silver shot from $6 an ounce to $32? "Silver fever" was the talk of the day; people were rushing to buy, including the two of us. We made a two-hour round trip to a silver dealer we knew, and we gave a little money for a bag of those precious coins. We bought for $23 an ounce; within several weeks silver was $7 an ounce. That dumb little bag is still lying in our safety deposit box.

But a friend of ours who's usually steady and wise sold his only real estate for silver—and soon had practically lost his life savings.

What was the matter with him and us? All three of us had misled faith. We'd put our confidence in something that didn't have staying power.

Here's an important principle: *Put your trust in things that last.*

And the longer a commodity's life—

And the more reliable the one who predicts that life—

The stronger can be your confidence.

This is all-important. There's a big difference between staying power and stubbornness—mulishness—hanging on for dear life to something false or transient or unworthy. Like silver. Like the Tooth Fairy.

We're talking now from eternity's viewpoint. Maybe in

heaven you'll thank us for writing this, because it got you putting your confidence in what counts most.

"The longer a commodity's life," we say, "and the more reliable the one who predicts that life, the stronger can be your confidence."

Then on what few things can you put your faith without wavering? Let's look at ultimates, at what will last forever, as predicted by the only final authority, God.

1. *You can put your faith in the Church. It has ultimate staying power.* Jesus prophesied that the gates of hell would not overcome it (see Matt. 16:18). The Spirit predicted "glory in the church . . . throughout all generations, for ever and ever! Amen" (Eph. 3:21).

The life of the Church, the functioning of the Church, the glory of God in the Church will go on and on and on. The Church has total staying power.

It's true that these verses are talking about the invisible, authentic Church, the body of Christ. But how can you relate to that Church except as it's expressed in the visible church—the "church of God in Corinth" or in Kansas City?

Then handle it with respect, with awe. God has vindicated it. Be careful how you criticize; the Church will never die; will you?

(Tourists in France were criticizing the Mona Lisa, and a gallery guard couldn't resist commenting, "Sir and madam, this painting is no longer a candidate for judgment. But you are.")

If you're smart, you'll speak only well of the Church. It may be that a local assembly may become so decadent, you will delicately, quietly, humbly transfer elsewhere. But be careful to make it your practice to love and respect and support and be part of "the Church." The Church rolls on forever, like a tank, crushing those who oppose it, and bearing within itself its own scars and the glory of a redeeming, vindicating God.

Don't be too bugged by the worldwide church's temporary sidetracks and divisions and foolishnesses. Whatever they are, let your love for the Church have staying power. God's does.

2. *You can put your faith in the Bible. It, too, has ultimate staying power.* Every generation hears a reincarnation of the serpent's words in the Garden, some new twist of doctrine which questions, "Did God really say . . . ?" (see Gen. 3:1).

Settle it once and for all, that you will trust the Bible. You may not *understand* something that seems like an apparent inconsistency. Well, why shouldn't God write something larger than can be grasped totally by one peanut mind?

As the heavens are higher than the earth,
so are my ways higher than your ways
and my thoughts than your thoughts (Isa. 55:9),

says God. Know that the "thoughts of God," in the only book He has recorded them in, have challenged and awed the greatest minds of every generation.

But you can "bet your last dollar" on the Bible. You can, you must, personally rely on the Word of God. It joins the Church in the list of things that have ultimate staying power:

Your word, O LORD, is eternal;
it stands firm in the heavens (Ps. 119:89).

Look, when you're choosing what to put your confidence in, what to give your closest attention to, let it be the Scriptures over the finest real estate. "Heaven and earth will pass away," says Christ, "but my words will never pass away" (Mark 13:31).

It will guide you (Ps. 119:105).
It will keep you from sin (Ps. 119:11).
It will be your delight (Ps. 1:2).
It will equip you for every good work (2 Tim. 3:16–17).

It will comfort and renew you (Ps. 119:50).
It will give you staying power (Ps. 119:92)!

3. *You can also put your faith in your coming C Zone, God's future inheritance for you.* What is it we believers are going to get later on? Nobody knows. It's a surprise. But we know it will be wonderful, and we know it also will have ultimate staying power:

In his great mercy [God] has given us new birth into a living hope . . . and into an inheritance that can never perish, spoil or fade—kept in heaven for you, who through faith are shielded by God's power until the coming of the salvation that is ready to be revealed in the last time (1 Pet. 1:3–5).

Don't think of your "salvation" as only a past or present experience; brother, you ain't seen nothin' yet. The salvation waiting to be revealed is God's glorious wrap-up, His conclusion, His punch line.

Whatever it is you've become heir to, it's prepared and waiting. "Through faith" you are being kept for it, and it is being kept for you.

"Through faith." The Bible seems to indicate that the gift is, if anything, more sure than you are; it seems only to be contingent on your faith, your staying power:

If you continue in your faith, established and firm, not moved from the hope held out in the gospel (Col. 1:23).

You need to persevere so that when you have done the will of God, you will receive what he has promised (Heb. 10:36).

So don't put misled faith into things that will fail you. Listen: *your life will absorb the quality of that which occupies you.* If you're wrapped up in the superficial, you'll be superficial, too. If you're occupied with that which has depth and staying power—you'll have staying power too.

4. *You can put your trust in the Source of all staying power, God Himself.*

What a God!

Moses asked Him what His name was, and He answered, "I AM."

> "I AM." Simple. Direct. Unequivocal. There is no hesitation, no hint of not-having-quite-arrived, no exaggeration.
>
> "I AM." Positive. Assured. Self-validated. He is alive and well, and not to be questioned.
>
> "I AM." Current. Continuous. There is no apology, no explanation, no contextualizing.
>
> "I AM." Complete. Self-contained. Secure. . . .
>
> "I AM." Unique. Other. Transcendent.
>
> "I AM." What He is, He is; what He chooses to be, He will be. . . . He is THE NAME: "I AM."[1]

And centuries after He gave us that Name, He stooped to reveal Himself in terms we better understand: time terms. He said, I am He "who is, and who was, and who is to come" (Rev. 1:4).

He was explaining to us, "My dear children, in relation to you, I have My own A Zone, B Zone, and C Zone. I began everything in perfection. But then came the great struggle between righteousness and evil, and the pain of the incarnation and the cross. But I will persevere until sin is utterly defeated and you are released. And then I shall be All in All—and I in you and you in Me, in perfect union and fellowship.

"So I understand your past and your present and your future. I identify with you in each. And I have ultimate staying power: I am the same yesterday, today, and forever."

Let your life be settled on these four great sureties, more than on any other supports or concerns: on the Church, on the Bible, on your future, and on God Himself.

1. Source unknown.

Now, why should we say such obvious, rock-bottom, kindergarten-level truths to you?

Because we're all a little cuckoo. "All we like sheep have gone astray" (Isa. 53:6). We all have tendencies to get off course, to major on the minors, to get excited over some lesser doctrine, to put our energies into some passing fad, to stake our last dollar on some quirk, some idiosyncrasy—the shaky and the flaky.

Life is full of land mines! As the Bible says in Ephesians 5:15, "See, then, that you walk circumspectly"—which means, keep looking around before you put your foot down. There's a lot of the shaky and the flaky around you.

What are some specific things you might steer clear of? Well, here are two, for starters:

1. *Beware of public movements that stem from fear.* In the early 1960s, fear drove multitudes of Christians in America into such a panic over Communism that many Christian leaders were suddenly suspect. Huge "Christian" rallies were held to alert people to the danger, and they got believers everywhere playing detective, sniffing under every bush and tree to ferret out pastors who might be part of the plot to turn us over to the Russians. Many innocent pastors were hurt. Including us.

Shortly after came the presidential contest between John F. Kennedy and Richard M. Nixon. Now it wasn't the Communists, it was the Catholic church. Fear gripped a lot more believers that Mr. Kennedy was scheming with the Pope to put the country under Catholic power. The last week before the election, two prominent Christian leaders sent telegrams to hundreds of us pastors over the country, urging us to publicly persuade our congregations to vote for Mr. Nixon. They said we were in all-out war against the devil, and we must stand for righteousness.

In the long perspective, that advice turned out to be a little shaky and flaky. We're glad now that we didn't advise our people at all.

A few years after that, a good man who should have known better stood up in our midweek prayer meeting to expose a sinister government plot. He showed us two one-dollar bills, one imprinted with the words "In God we trust," and the other, not.

"Do you realize," he said, "that our federal government has just quietly removed these words from our dollar bills? This is part of their atheistic, humanistic scheme to get rid of God, and I urge you to sign this paper tonight to object. Let's storm Washington with millions of signatures!" Almost everybody signed.

Within days we discovered it was the *new* dollar bills that included the words "In God we trust," and Washington had recently put them *on*.

2. *Beware of financial temptations*. The best way to get money is still payday by payday. As Proverbs 13:11 says, "He who gathers money little by little makes it grow."

There's a lot of the shaky and the flaky in financial deals.

Years ago a really distinguished Christian came to us hoping we'd invest in a wonderful deal with him. He was known over the country for his good works, and his reputation was excellent. He was going to put Christians' money into a little company that would mushroom overnight as it produced 3-D pictures of Jesus in garish colors that glowed in the dark. Our money would come back, he said, many times over.

We looked at those pictures. We said to each other, "Jesus in 3-D? He glows in the dark?" We decided it was shaky and flaky, and we said no.

Sadly, many pastors and Christian workers invested

in that thing, and when it went under, they lost lots of money, and the man committed suicide.

More recently a wonderful young fellow asked us to be guarantors of a loan for him. Why didn't we remember that Proverbs 22:26,27 says never to do that? We wanted to encourage him, and we signed. When his little company bellied up, the bank came after us and really cleaned us out. We didn't pray about that, and that's why we missed our cue that it was shaky and flaky.

First Peter 4:19 gives the most obvious advice for staying power: "Continue to do good." We might say, "Well, of course; why say something so obvious?"

But, no, the two of us are taking that verse literally, humbly, soberly. We feel our together-ministry of speaking and writing will be validated if God will help us, as long as we live, to stay married, avoid doctrinal excesses, keep our finances honest and careful—"continue to do good," as best we know how.

It's not so much if we write with flair or speak with charisma. Sometimes we see contemporaries dear to us, with twice our gifts, go down in balls of flames.

The two of us are committed to steering clear of the shaky and the flaky. We are capable of blowing it all! But we want, God helping us, to keep in order our family life, our material possessions, our relationships, and our ministry. Fred Smith says that "good teachers personify their message."

Oh, pray for us, that God will protect us from our own selves—our weaknesses, our blindnesses, our stupidities; that we will fix our eyes on Jesus and never discredit the glorious Gospel.

You want that, too, don't you?

Well, let's walk "circumspectly." For staying power in good, long lives, let's look around before we put our foot down. Let's steer clear of the shaky and the flaky.

Never buy
a portable TV set
on a sidewalk
from a man
who's out
of breath

CHAPTER 17

Staying Power for Your Marriage

"Why don't we get along?" we sang to each other for years. It's a jazzy little song, and we sang it good-humoredly, but we also sang it because there was truth in it:

> Why don't we get along?
> Ever'thing I do is wrong—
> Tell me, what's the reason
> I'm not pleasin'
> You?

How could we know we were in the B Zone? We hadn't even thought up the term yet!

We only knew that we were two strong people who often clashed, and that in the beginning it hadn't been so. And that was not only uncomfortable, it was discouraging—because we supposed that the rest of our marriage would be more of the same.

We didn't know that every marriage has its B Zone; and more than that, we didn't know that B Zones aren't forever—that if we "hung in there" and sought to work through our problems, a C Zone would surely come.

In fairy tales, when the prince and the princess get married, they live happily ever after. They go straight from the A Zone to the C Zone.

Outside of fairy tales, nobody's ever done that. But young marrieds, full of idealism like us, hurt because they suppose their B Zone is replacing their C Zone! They assume they simply have a less-than-good marriage.

What a pity! Adolescents know their pimples and braces aren't forever, but young couples think their irritations and imcompatibilities are. Yet both can be just stages of B Zones.

How helpful it is to see yourself in marriage in part of a process!

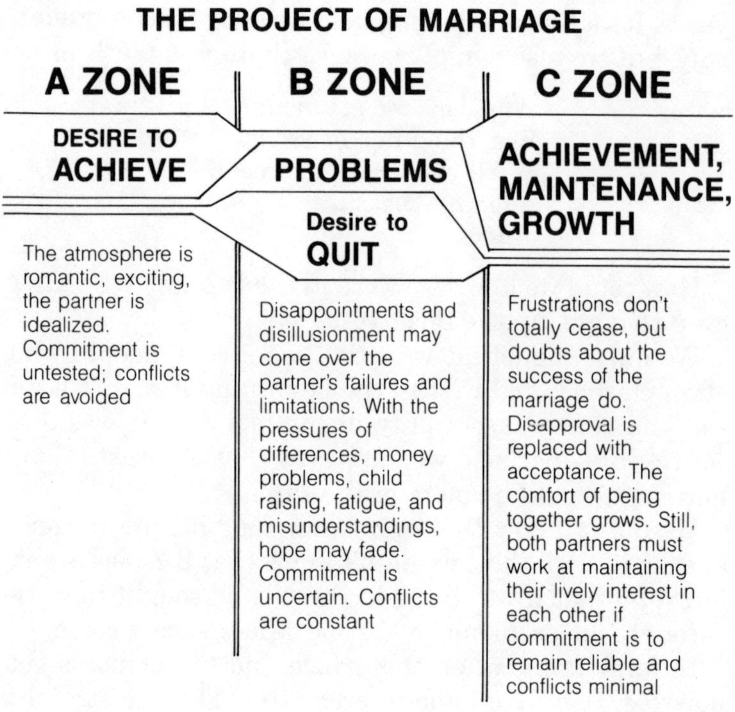
THE PROJECT OF MARRIAGE
A ZONE
B ZONE
C ZONE
DESIRE TO ACHIEVE
PROBLEMS
ACHIEVEMENT, MAINTENANCE, GROWTH
Desire to QUIT
The atmosphere is romantic, exciting, the partner is idealized. Commitment is untested; conflicts are avoided
Disappointments and disillusionment may come over the partner's failures and limitations. With the pressures of differences, money problems, child raising, fatigue, and misunderstandings, hope may fade. Commitment is uncertain. Conflicts are constant
Frustrations don't totally cease, but doubts about the success of the marriage do. Disapproval is replaced with acceptance. The comfort of being together grows. Still, both partners must work at maintaining their lively interest in each other if commitment is to remain reliable and conflicts minimal

The Bible says that your need is to hang in there.

You need to persevere so that when you have done the will of God, you will receive what he has promised (Heb. 10:36).

Indeed, we count them blessed who endure (James 5:11).

Blessed is the man who perseveres under trial, because when he has stood the test, he will receive the crown of life that God has promised to those who love him (James 1:12).

At the risk of not saying enough about how to endure, how to persevere, in your marriage (our entire book *Building a Great Marriage*[1] was written to do just that), let's talk about the threats to that perseverance. There are four major threats, as we see them:

1. *The temptation to criticize and get hostile with each other.* The solution begins inside yourself. George Mueller used to say, "The first great and primary business to which I must attend every day is to see that my soul is happy in the Lord." This means keeping your heart in direct communication with Him. Think of yourself as a deep-sea diver. You're in a foreign environment in this world, but you stay well because of your vital and constant connection with an upper region!

Chapter Fifteen suggested for you other disciplines, but here let's suggest the discipline, the "holy habit," of inner confession and worship, while you go about your day.

Confession is taking the low position for yourself. As soon as you're aware of a wrong thought or deed, mentally rush to Him, saying, "Father, I sinned! I did so-and-so. Forgive me; I'm sorry. Help me not to do it again."

Worship is lifting Him up. Seek to "practice his presence," and admire Him continually in your heart. As

1. Anne Ortlund, *Building a Great Marriage* (Old Tappan, N.J.: Fleming H. Revell, 1985).

you work, as you live, keep a conversation with Him going inside you! Try this little formula, "Lord, You are ______," and fill in the blank: "Lord, You are my Shepherd. Lord, You are the Bread of Life. Lord, You are holy. Lord, You are patient with me. . . ."

Now, at the same time you're working on these two inner disciplines, work on two outer ones which correlate: apologizing to your partner and affirming your partner.

Apologizing is taking the low position for yourself.[2] As soon as you're aware of something negative between you, be the first to accept blame:

"Honey, I didn't mean to bug you. . . ."

"Did I blow it?"

"Boy, I shouldn't have said that. I knew it as soon as it was out of my mouth. . . ."

Take the low approach! Expect to be saying "I'm sorry" many times "as long as you both shall live."

Affirming is lifting up your partner. Say it in words, over and over:

"You are so wonderful!"

"I love you so much."

"I was so proud of you tonight. . . ."

Often be specific:

"I love your sense of humor."

"You have the nicest hands. . . ."

Do you see how the pair of inner disciplines are actively using the same muscles as the pair of outer disciplines?

The two of us know that when we begin to criticize or get hostile with each other, it's because we're not right on the inside.

"Get rid of all bitterness, rage and anger, brawling

2. See Anne Ortlund, *Children Are Wet Cement* (Old Tappan, N.J.: Fleming H. Revell, 1981), pp. 105–113.

and slander, along with every form of malice" says Ephesians 4:31. (Don't express it, which hurts your spouse; don't suppress it, which hurts you; put it away from you, *get rid of it*—through the salvation which is in Jesus Christ.) "Be kind and compassionate to one another, forgiving each other, just as in Christ God forgave you" (Eph. 4:32).

The first temptation, the temptation to criticize and get hostile with each other, if yielded to, will lead to the second temptation. (When your spouse begins to look bad to you, someone else will start to look good.)

2. *The temptation to that first unfaithfulness.*

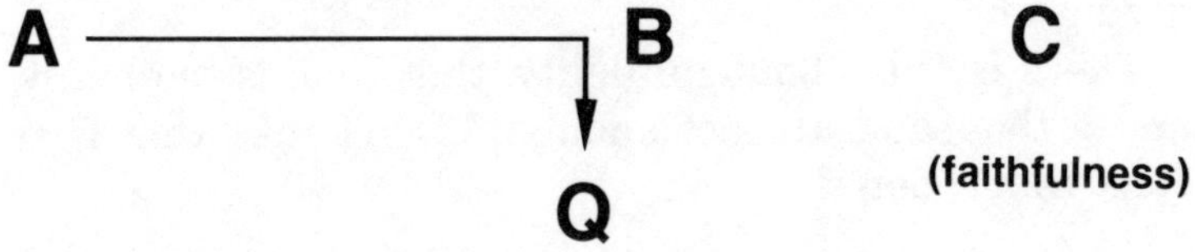

This temptation stalks the streets, and Proverbs 7:6–23 says it barrages all our senses:

Sight: "Then out came a woman to meet him, dressed like a prostitute and with crafty intent."

Touch: "She took hold of him and kissed him."

Appeal to the ego: "With a brazen face she said: / '. . . I came out to meet you; I looked for you and have found you!'"

Smell: "'I have perfumed my bed. . . .'"

Sound: "With persuasive words she led him astray; she seduced him with her smooth talk."

Then—

> All at once he followed her
> like an ox going to the slaughter,
> like a deer stepping into a noose
> till an arrow pierces his liver,

like a bird darting into a snare,
little knowing it will cost him his life.

Reader, if you're tempted to your first infidelity, hear this strong word from us:

Commitment in marriage has great payoffs. To know that you have been faithful "to her alone," "to him alone," as you originally vowed, will be a wonderful, comforting, stabilizing knowledge in your C Zone. (Live with your future in mind!)

Once you break that marriage commitment, it's *broken*. Understand that. You don't "break it once," you *break* it. Like a chain, it's either broken or it's not broken. When you're tempted, think about what you'd be giving up!

There is this about infidelity, that "one is too many, and a thousand are not enough." Don't take that first step. Don't, don't!

3. *The temptation to continued unfaithfulness*. Maybe for you, the chain is already broken. The pattern, the cycle has been established, and it's hard to stop. . . .

It's true that your body doesn't want to be monogamous. But you're not a mere body, an animal. Then hear the word of God, and let your mind and your spirit decide from now on to rule over your body:

Abstain . . . from sexual immorality (Acts 15:20).

The body is not for sexual immorality, but for the Lord (1 Cor. 6:13).

The acts of the sinful nature are obvious: sexual immorality, impurity and debauchery; idolatry and witchcraft; hatred, discord, jealousy, fits of rage, selfish ambition, dissensions, factions and envy; drunkenness, orgies, and the like. I warn you, as I did before, that those who live like this will not inherit the kingdom of God (Gal. 5:19–21).

Perhaps you need to find a minister, gather a few friends as witnesses, and repeat your wedding vows again!

4. *The temptation to divorce.*

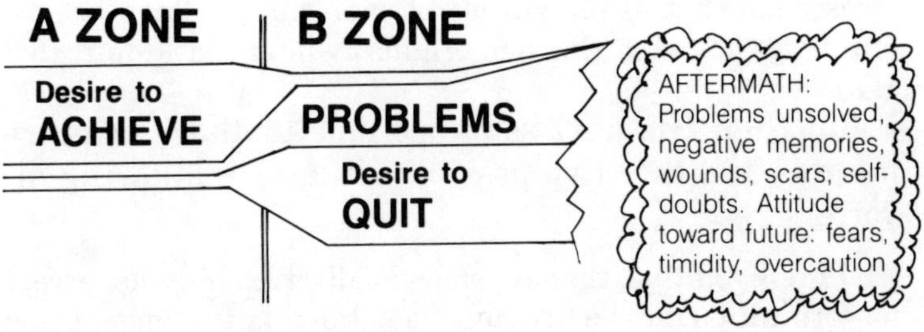

Never mind what big shots are doing it; know what the Bible says about it.

God says in Malachi 2:16 that He hates divorce. It doesn't say He hates divorced *people*—no, no—but He hates divorce because of what it does in ripping and tearing up and damaging His precious children.

Is divorce ever allowable according to the Scriptures? When the Pharisees asked Jesus if it was lawful for a man to divorce his wife, He answered with great strength,

> "Don't you read the Scriptures?" he replied. "In them it is written that at the beginning God created man and woman, and that a man should leave his father and mother, and be forever united to his wife. The two shall become one—no longer two, but one! And no man may divorce what God has joined together" (Matt. 19:4–6 TLB).

But when Jesus seemed so adamant against divorce, the Pharisees pressed him, as people are still apt to do:

"Then, why," they asked, "did Moses say a man may divorce his wife by merely writing her a letter of dismissal?" (Matt. 19:7 TLB).

Jesus' answer shows how loath He was to make divorce seem a logical solution:

> "Moses did that in recognition of your hard and evil hearts, but it was not what God had originally intended" (Matt. 19:8 TLB).

But then His next sentence and another Scripture later on indicate two possible situations allowing divorce:

> And I tell you this, that anyone who divorces his wife, except for fornication [or the NIV says "marital unfaithfulness"], and marries another, commits adultery (Matt. 19:9 TLB).

Opening the door a crack, "except for fornication," is vastly different from throwing it open wide. He didn't say, "Now, all of you who have been cheated on, please feel free to walk right on through here. There's no problem. You've got your ticket to divorce right in your hand. Y'all come!"

The implication is, "If you insist, it's permissible for this reason, but don't feel you must. Forgiving, persevering, loving is better."

Permanent desertion by a non-Christian partner from a Christian partner is the second possibility. Again, when the Bible brings this up, it presents it not as a free ticket to exit a marriage, but as a very last resort:

> If any brother has a wife who is an unbeliever, and she consents to live with him, he should not divorce her. If any woman has a husband who is an unbeliever, and he consents to live with her, she should not divorce him. For the unbelieving husband is consecrated through his wife, and the unbelieving wife is consecrated through her husband. Otherwise, your children would be unclean, but as it is they are holy (1 Cor. 7:12b–14 TLB).

God is concerned about the welfare of the children. Let's go back to our diagram of aborting a project, and see that the marriage situation is unique in one particular way. The cloud of "aftermath" becomes like an atomic cloud, with the lethal fallout on the children:

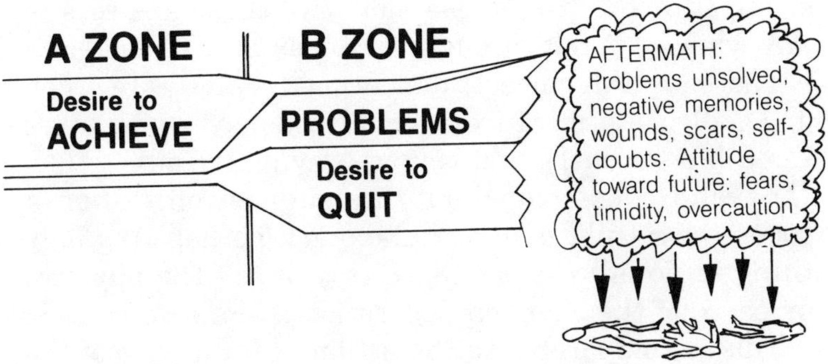

Recently we heard a radio talk show psychologist spend a lengthy period of time interviewing only adults in their thirties and beyond whose parents had divorced many years before, when they were children.

All of these adults interviewed had either never married or they had married and divorced several times, and the same reason came through repeatedly like a broken record: a whole generation later, these people could not successfully relate to adults in a close, trusting situation because of an unshakable fear that they might be abandoned.

This is not to discourage you if you're the child of divorced parents; the power of the Holy Spirit can make glorious exceptions to every human tendency! This is a warning to couples considering divorce.

Remember the cloud. Miles and years later . . . there may still be fallout.

But gentle people who are thinking about the hurt of

bad marriages may be asking, "What if the relationship gets actually violent, or if the marriage is just too miserable to stay intact?"

Do we qualify to answer that—we who have never suffered in this way? In counseling others we have hurt when they hurt, but it's not the same. We don't want to sound flippant or give easy one-two-three answers to any who are going through very deep marital waters.

There are three needs. Repentance is always in order, and godly counseling from a qualified person who takes the Bible seriously, and loving, praying friends.

Beyond those, consider this suggestion: When a spouse or a child is in actual danger, perhaps the only thing to do is to separate, to stay out of the physical presence of the offender. Separation is not divorce.

This is comparable to the action of the father of the prodigal son. The father let him go and put physical distance between them, but he didn't disown his son. He didn't cut him off. He was saying, "I haven't changed. I'm still on the same old terms, ready to receive you again. When you repent and return, my love for you will have persevered through it all. I'll be right there, welcoming you back, eagerly and forever."

There are many marriages today of great triumph, in which one partner has remained patient and faithful and forgiving in spite of every legitimate reason for divorce, until the erring partner repents.

Elizabeth Achtemeier writes of her own parents in her book *The Committed Marriage,*

> To give a personal witness, I grew up in a home which, for a period, was marked with violent differences, arguments, and the threat of divorce. Through all the turbulence and heartache, my Christian mother refused to agree to the separation because she thought it was wrong for a Christian to do so. Some outside of the family thought she was foolish, but personally I am deeply grateful to her. Contrary to the belief of

some psychologists, she prevented psychic damage to her children far beyond what measure of it we suffered in a troubled home. She lived to enjoy a mellowed and loving relationship with Dad in their later years. He himself came to a simple but deep Christian faith, and the last words I heard Mother say to him before her death were, "You really do love me, don't you?"[3]

If Elizabeth's mother hadn't had staying power for that marriage, how would Elizabeth have turned out? Do you think that a generation later that wonderful book would ever have been written, to the blessing of many?

Let us tell you about two real couples (their names are, of course, changed) among our friends.

1. Susie has been married to Kevin for fifteen years. She and Kevin are both attractive, prominent Christians, and they have five beautiful children. Many younger believers have looked to them as models, and they are pillars in their church.

Recently Susie was shocked to discover that Kevin had been playing around with another woman. Susie is divorcing him.

2. Jane became a believer early in her marriage, and she faithfully loved and cared for her husband Carey through insult after insult as he flirted openly before her and had affair after affair. This behavior went on for thirty years!

But Jane had staying power: Her love simply outlasted Carey's rebellion. And when at last he was broken and repentant and accepted Christ into his heart, he couldn't appreciate and love her enough.

Look at these two marriages from the perspective of ten years from now. (Remember, keep your eyes ahead, and always live today in the light of tomorrow.)

3. Philadelphia: Westminster Press, 1976, p. 127.

1. Susie and Kevin will have bitter memories locked inside their hearts, and damaged children, and friends who never understood and so backed away. There could be awkward children's weddings. . . . They themselves may also have new marriages and the confusion of relationships between ex-spouses and current ones, "his" children and "hers," and too many grandparents, uncles, and aunts, mostly also hurting and confused. They'll have rethought whether they could remain in their church, and probably one will have left, feeling abandoned and resentful. Both will feel uncertain about their "ministries" (they've been Bible teachers) for the rest of their lives, in the church's confusion over whether they still qualify for leadership and service.

2. Jane and Carey will be in their "golden years," considered by their church as models—a lovely older couple who had earlier struggles but finally "made it." And Carey, in great gratitude, will probably treat Jane as he does today—like the queen that she truly is.

How should you act in your B Zone? The way you'll be glad you did when you look back from your C Zone. Keep your eyes on the future! It will shape the present you.

Listen: In your marriage, as in every marriage, there will be, along the way, those little—enormous!—moments of decision when you take a stand, one way or the other:

"I will forgive" (Matt. 18:21–22), or—

"I will not forgive."

The great Napoleon said this: "In every battle there is a crisis of perhaps ten to fifteen minutes on which the outcome depends. The proper use of that short period means victory. Improper use of those few minutes, and one is destined for defeat."

Amazing!

Expect along the way those ten-to-fifteen minute crises, and decide right now that your love will not be conditional; as often as the crises come, you will forgive and forgive and forgive.

And do you know what? Chances are, you will also be forgiven.

Begin, persevere in your marriage, win!

Happy fiftieth anniversary, in advance!

Of all
the sad words
on the loose,
the saddest
are these:
"Oh, what's the use?"

CHAPTER 18

Staying Power in Your Singleness

More and more, it's a singles' world.

One-half the average congregation, from high schoolers on up, is single.

There are more singles buying homes and new cars than ever before, and singles take three times as many vacation trips as other adults.

(We just got a postcard from two friends who are single gals. They're touring New England this summer, and they wrote, "We're here on a religious expedition. We're fishing for men!")

Roughly a quarter of all United States households are people living alone, and some other countries report an even higher count. For single parents there are special problems, and the need is great to relate deeply to a congregation so that the physical family which is partial can become whole in the spiritual family.[1]

The commercial world has discovered that the growing single population is a group to be catered to—from one- and two-bedroom condos to one-cup teapots and single hot dog steamers!

Let's think about the spiritual needs of singles.

For divorcees the new single life is filled with all the aftermath of an aborted B Zone. Painful!

1. See Anne Ortlund, *Discipling One Another* (Waco, Tex.: Word, 1979).

For widowed people the grieving may go on until it becomes chronic regret, with the formed habit of looking backward instead of onward, and with the inevitable result of beginning to die inside.

For never-married singles there may be the feeling of an unending B Zone, a life less than fulfilled. These people may think of a some-day marriage as an immediate C Zone, the end of all their problems, in which they'd live happily ever after. They need to understand that the single life has its own A, B, and C Zones, just as any future marriage would have its own A, B, and C Zones.

For the situation of singleness there is the A Zone, the early stage when there are so many around you like yourself and probably you imagine that your singleness won't last long.

Then, typically, there's the B Zone, when you're "always a bridesmaid, never a bride," and your world seems to shrink, relationally. There are fewer single friends left (perhaps fewer *friends*, since "wedding bells are breaking up that old gang of mine"), fewer dates, and fewer prospective marriage partners around. But you have more loneliness, more holiday seasons when you feel depressed, and more situations when you feel, even for practical reasons, incomplete because you need someone of the opposite sex.

There's a further reason for being depressed as a single when you're a Christian. Whereas singles of the world may "swing" and live it up socially and feel there's no stigma anymore to the single life (never mind the threat of venereal diseases and all the psychological neuroses), you feel plenty of stigma. Your local church may simply "use" you, squeezing all the service out of you it can get; or the members may look on you as a freak and not know where to fit you in—or not *attempt* to fit you in; or they may shunt you off to a singles' group which is nothing more than a "meet" market; and you are taught by implication that because the husband pictures Christ and the wife pictures the Church, you really *are* sort of spiritually second class.

There's much to battle, and for this situation we highly recommend (forgive our lack of modesty) our book *Discipling One Another*,[2] which gives advice to singles and to the local church on how to mesh together and function within the true body of Christ.

But a good C Zone can come unexpectedly, perhaps: when you tackle the problems or come to terms with them one by one, and you adjust. You discover that the single life is good, that there are many advantages, and that you're thankful for God's choice for you—at least for the present.

You become more aggressive in nourishing friendships in your life. You get into a small group for accountability and for spiritual and emotional feeding (connectedness was never more important). You discover things you like to do, to replace your previously fuller date life. You help improve the quality of your singles' Sunday school class, or else you get into another adult class where you find that there are more and more singles among the couples, anyway.

If you're widowed or divorced, you consciously end the excessive backward looking and the grieving, and you determine to set new goals and concentrate on the future.

And in all, you learn to trust God that His way for you is best, and you practice the discipline of continual thankfulness. . . . Yes, then your single life goes into the C Zone.

In your singleness, as long as God ordains it, *begin, persevere through the difficulties, and win!*

2. Ibid.

"Lord,
help us to remember
that we are only
limited
by all
that you are"

—Major Ian Thomas

CHAPTER 19

Staying Power for All Your Relationships

We had a phone call recently. She said her name was Trish, and she'd read one of our books, and she'd like some counseling over the phone. Trish said she'd just withdrawn her three children from a Christian school: "You would not believe what that principal said to me! I've never been so hurt. I wrote a letter right away and took out all three of my kids. The only thing he understands is money, and if his business goes down, he'll see he can't treat people that way and get by with it."

Then she said, "Sundays are weird for me because a woman in our church lied to me and took away a job I was doing, and I couldn't believe it—all the other women backed her up. They're all a bunch of hypocrites, and I just couldn't face them any more. So I changed churches, but my husband and the kids won't leave the other place, so I have to go alone."

She rambled into another story: "When I put my kids in public school, I joined a car pool here in the neighborhood, but I'm kind of nervous driving and I don't mind doing it if there's another adult in the car; and they all got mad at me for the simple reason that I wanted one of them with me, so I said, 'Forget your dumb car pool! It's not that far, and my kids can walk. . . .'"

Trish is willing to *begin* relationships, but she has no

staying power, and her "people world" is continually shrinking.

She reminds us of a little poem:

Then here's to you,
  And here's to me,
And may we never
  Disagree.
But if we do—
Then nuts to you,
  And here's to me!

Are you identifying with Trish? Do you make friends for a while and then lose them, and make more friends and somehow lose them—and the pattern keeps repeating? Like this—

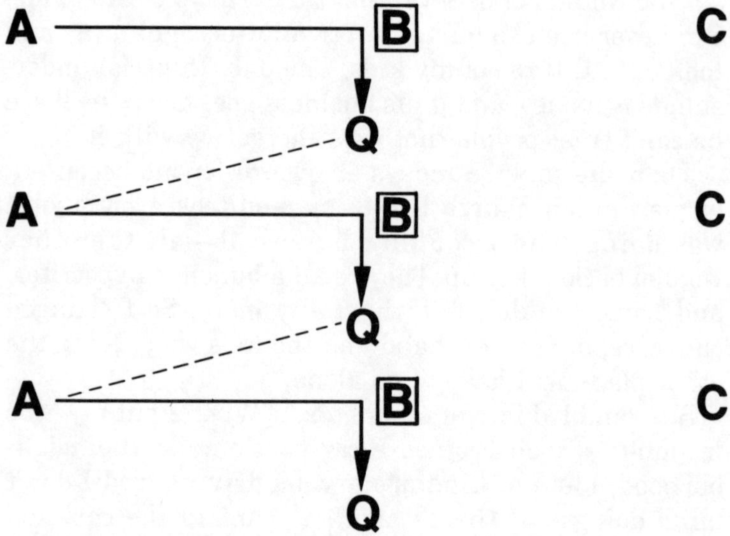

"It's not good for man to be alone," said God—and He meant that for you as well. You need relationships in your life that have depth and commitment.

Napoleon Bonaparte thought he needed only power. "I

make servants," he said; "I never pretend to make friends." And he died on a Mediterranean island, broken, alone, and powerless.

What can you do to develop relationships that have staying power?

1. *Choose someone going the same direction you are.* "Do two walk together unless they have agreed to do so?" (Amos 3:3). If you're headed toward Christ and the other person isn't, don't expect compatibility. You can't link arms and then head for opposite horizons.

2. *Choose someone you admire and want to copy.* That's what put David and Jonathan together.

Prince Jonathan, heir to the throne of Israel, was a young swashbuckling military hero. And out from the fields of battle came a young unknown with the bloody head of Goliath, the great enemy, in his hand! Jonathan's eyes must have popped out.

And General Abner—

> took him and brought him before [King] Saul, with David still holding the Philistine's head.
>
> "Whose son are you, young man?", Saul asked him.
>
> David said, "I am the son of your servant Jesse of Bethlehem."
>
> After David had finished talking with Saul, Jonathan became one in spirit with David, and he loved him as himself (1 Sam. 17:57–18:1).

And Jonathan and David copied each other, which is always the powerful effect of a close friendship.

You will become like your friend—so choose carefully. "He who walks with the wise grows wise, but a companion of fools suffers harm" (Prov. 13:20).

3. *Give the friendship plenty of time.* Jonathan and David at first, in a sense, selected each other; but given

time and exposure, God put them together. As the verse above says, their souls were knit together.

It takes time for a sweater to be knit, or for a broken bone to knit, and it takes time for friendships to knit. You have to have the time, and you have to be willing to give it. Don't let your lifestyle be too fast-paced for deep friendships.

In Colossians 2 Paul prayed for that body of believers to be knit together in love. Let it also be happening to you.

4. *Expect to give away a lot of yourself.*

And Jonathan made a covenant with David because he loved him as himself. Jonathan took off the robe he was wearing and gave it to David, along with his tunic, and even his sword, his bow and his belt (1 Sam. 18:3–4).

Remember, what Jonathan was giving David was his insignia of royalty, the signs that he was heir apparent to the throne. He was saying, "David, all that I have is yours." In a deep, prophetic way which Jonathan himself didn't understand until later, his gifts were saying, "I am not going to be king, David; you are. I am willing. I put you before myself. I step aside."

You, too, need at least one, maybe several, friends for whom you are willing to strip yourself—of your time, your money, your convenience, your energy, your loyalty. A worthy friendship should cost you plenty.

5. *When your relationship is threatened, know the biblical thing to do.* Eventually any sustained effort, including a friendship, will hit its own "midlife crisis," its B Zone. When it comes, what do you do?

If you're the one who goofed, Matthew 5:23,24 says it's your move first. If your friend is the one who goofed, Matthew 18:15 says it's still your move first.

In other words, no matter whose fault it was, it's always your move.

And what do you do? You go to him and talk it over, one on one (see Matt. 5:24; 18:15).

This is key, it's scriptural, it's right.

Don't tell anyone else. Don't grouse around and spread the problem and force others to take sides. Protect your reputation and his by talking it over privately. "If he listens to you, you have won your brother over" (Matt. 18:15), and you've pumped staying power into your relationship.

If that doesn't help, then Matthew says to take one or two others to help the two of you solve the problem (see 18:16).

Then if that doesn't bring a solution, "tell it to the church" (18:17)—probably to official leaders, to spiritual elders with good common sense. Does that sound too radical? Probably Step Three would almost never be needed if the first two steps were faithfully followed.

6. *Manage your relationships from the viewpoint of your C Zone.* Before you're ever tempted to say or do something impulsive, something negative, stop and think. *Will this contribute toward a solid future relationship with this person? Is it a building block toward a C Zone?*

Solid, understanding relationships are precious; they'll do you good all your life. When you're onto the possibility of one, handle with care.

7. *Love your friends with unconditional love.* "Receive one another, just as Christ also received us" (Rom. 15:7)—scars, warts, and all! Unless we receive each other that way, no deep friendships will ever emerge.

Sometimes your friend will be at less than his best. Maybe he's out of adrenalin, out of cope. A good friend knows how, at that point, to separate what he says from what he means.

When Elijah was out of strength and patience, he blurted out, "God, let me die!" If the Lord had answered his prayer, Elijah would have missed his whole friendship with Elisha, plus years of wonderful ministry, plus being caught up to heaven in a chariot of fire!

Fortunately for Elijah, God was his good friend who knew how to recognize when Elijah was giving Him baloney, and He didn't take him seriously.

Unconditional love says, "You can't say or do anything that would change my relationship with you. Period."

Years ago there were tensions between Chile and Argentina. At last they came to their senses and made a covenant of friendship. To commemorate their friendship, the two countries erected that glorious statue "The Christ of the Andes" and inscribed on it these words:

> Sooner shall these mountains crumble to dust than Chile and Argentina shall break the peace they have made at the feet of the Redeemer.

Begin friendships, persevere in them, and win!

"The richest man in the world is not the one who still has the first dollar he ever earned. It's the man who still has his first friend"

—Martha Mason, quoted by Sid Archer in the Egg Harbor, N.J. *News*

CHAPTER 20

Walk So You Leave Behind Good Footprints

Think C Zone! Live each day so that later on you'll look back with satisfaction.

You can do that! You can't manage your circumstances, but you can manage *how you react* to your circumstances. Remember, living is between your ears!

So from this moment on, God helping you, if you choose, you can do two things to leave behind good footprints.

1. *Start building for yourself the memories you want when you look back tomorrow.*

Two women sat next to us recently in a restaurant. When our conversation lulled, we realized they were discussing handling their teenage sons.

"Well," said one, "it's not always easy. But my husband is so wise. He says, 'Trina, say or do in such a way that you'll feel good about it later on, when you look back.'"

We said this to a couple at a conference recently. They hadn't been married too long, and they had "his" children and "her" children under one roof, and they were going so crazy that they were thinking about splitting.

"Look," we said, "think about down the road. Don't just get a little temporary relief by divorcing and then have years of regret forever after.

"So it's bad now. But when the children are gone,

you'll be so glad you hung in together. The children cause temporary stress, but you have the great privilege of a permanent marriage. Outlast them!"

Think C Zone! Build now the memories you want when you look back tomorrow.

At another conference a while back at a really wonderful church, the assistant pastor's wife took us aside for a little confidential chat.

"Pray with us," she said, "that Charles [the senior pastor] will move on. There are a lot of people in this church, including us, who feel the church has outgrown him, and we need a fresh start."

Now, the senior pastor of that church was a godly, humble, beautiful man who had come ten years earlier when the church was nothing and had brought it to its current strong, basically healthy condition (although in the last year there had been a ground swell of criticism and opposition).

With all the fervor in our bones we said, "Look, dear April, we don't know all the details of your situation, and neither do we know Charles deeply and well.

"But we believe whether you stay in this church or move on elsewhere, or whether Charles stays here or moves on—if you've been utterly loving and loyal to Charles, praying for him, encouraging him, maximizing his good points to others and quietly covering and filling in, where you can, for his weaknesses—if you've been that kind of assistant pastor and wife, you'll always feel good about it later on. You'll be glad you did. You won't lose.

"But if you murmur against him and join sides with others and let them murmur against him; or if you even simply 'damn him with faint praise' when he's on trial needing your defense and protection—in the long haul you could be terribly sorry. You could get caught in a mess that could damage your whole ministry career.

"Look down the road! Conduct yourselves each day in

the light of the future—in the way you want your career to give you the greatest pleasure as you look back."

April began to cry! She knew we were right. She and her husband are two wonderful people who, in fatigue, had lost perspective. We loved them too much not to stop them short.

Think C Zone! Build now the memories you want when you look back tomorrow. We could make it into a proverb: "Eat only what will leave a good taste in your mouth!"

2. *Start building, as well, other people's memories of you.* For instance, *speak your negative words, but write your positive ones.*

Don't put your negative feelings on paper! If you're distressed over people's actions, don't "write a letter." Pray first, perhaps take a wise third party, and go see them. When you're face to face, your touches and your tone of voice can soften what you say, and you can hear their side of it and maybe even reach an understanding.

(Incidentally, never, never write an anonymous letter. That's definitely shaky and flaky, and only shaky and flaky people in this world take them seriously.)

On the other hand, as often as possible write notes and letters of commendation and encouragement. Say them, yes—but also write them. Our friend Dr. Ted Engstrom does that, and he's much loved for it.

Think future! When you're dead and gone, you want to leave behind in this world not one bad piece of paper for people to find—but hundreds of good ones for them to remember you by.

And in everything you do, *live so they'll cry at your funeral.* Wouldn't you like some day to be really missed? Then "reach out and touch." Each smile of yours, each hug, each encouraging word could become a specific little memory in someone's mind later one. Why not?

Say it now, do it now while you can, to every person

you can—and build those memories. Stack 'em up for a great funeral!

Get perspective. Live from your C Zone backward.

Says Amy Carmichael, "We have all eternity to enjoy our rewards, but only a few short years to win them."

And God wants to do more than bring His sons to glory; He wants to bring glory to His sons! He wants to do more than bring your soul to heaven; He wants to bring heaven to your soul!

When you spend your life with future rewards in mind, your present life becomes rewarding as well. Build your own future memories, and build other people's future memories of you.

Walk so you leave behind good footprints.

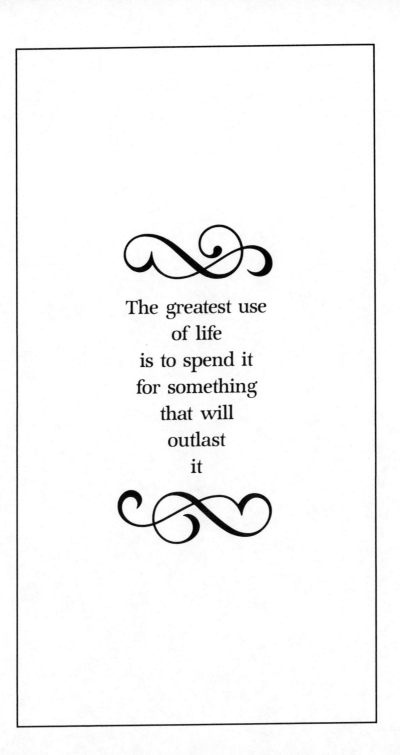

The greatest use
of life
is to spend it
for something
that will
outlast
it

CHAPTER 21

The Power to Live Well for a Long Time

ABC—ABC—ABC—ABC—ABC—ABC—ABC→

God forbid that this be a book on old age. But don't you think "staying power" includes how to stay young a long time?

Recently George Burns was given a party celebrating his eightieth anniversary of being in show business! "I'm delighted to be here," he said at the party, speaking about his life. "It's been fun so far; the other half should be just as good."

There's a profound principle here: *Stretch out your goals and expectations.*

George's party ended with a few final comments, like: "I'm going to stay in show business until I'm the only one left!"

Principle Two: *Choose creative work, and never quit.*

A young media fellow at Burns's party asked him if he could record him ten years from then. "Why not?" said George. "You should still be here."

Principle Three: *Forget yourself.*

Let's talk about each of these three principles for staying young a long time.

Principle One: *Stretch out your goals and expectations.*

A. *Plan 'way down the road.* Have dreams for twenty-five years from now, maybe fifty years from now.

You know very well that if you only have a morning project, at noon when you finish it you'll be pooped or bored. You'll probably just coast through the rest of the day.

But if you have something to do in the morning, and something else to do in the afternoon, and something else to do in the evening, your mind and body will stay humming all day, and there'll be purpose in your eye and sparkle in your step.

Don't have projects going for you only until you're sixty or seventy! When you finish them, you'll be literally "done," and from then on you'll start coasting. Don't die before you die! Says Robert Donovan, "Giving up is the ultimate tragedy."

Stretch out your expectations. Plan 'way down the road. The two of us, now age sixty-two, have said for a long time that, God willing, we're going to minister together in Renewal Ministries only until we're eighty-five, and after that (jokingly) we're going to fool around a while.

Well, before long we'd better set some after-eighty-five goals—exciting things that we don't have time to do now, and there are plenty of them. And those goals need to be as creative and others-centered and full of purpose and meaning as our present goals! Otherwise why take up earth's space and resources?

B. *Then pace yourself to last for those goals.*

Some people burn out at forty and are over the hill. Some people race through life at such a breakneck speed that at sixty-five they're finished. Some do it literally—and finish even sooner.

Burma Shave signs used to warn motorists about that:

Hardly a driver
Is now alive
Who passed on hills
At 75. Burma Shave.

Or—

He saw the train
And tried to duck it.
Kicked first the gas
And then the bucket. Burma Shave.

Or this one:

Her chariot raced
At 80 per;
They hauled away
What had Ben Hur. Burma Shave.

Terrible corn! But in other words, people who drive like there's no tomorrow may not have any.

Or workaholics who drive themselves.

Life is not a hundred-yard dash; it's a cross-country run. Live like it.

Stretching out your goals and pacing yourself to achieve them will keep you plenty busy enough! Said one very young grandmother at ninety, "It takes time to get old—and I've never had any."[1]

Here's the story of a man who set goals for himself and then paced himself to achieve them.

Caleb was one of twelve spies sent out by Moses to view the land of Canaan and bring back a report. Now, God had already done just that for them, and His report was that it was terrific (see Deut. 8:7–9). But He wanted them to see for themselves and agree with His assessment.

1. Vicentia Rogge, *Reader's Digest,* April 1984, p. 77.

You remember the spies' report. Ten said it was a great land, but the cities were fortified and the people such giants that the Israelites could never overcome them (see Num. 13:31–33).

(Actually, the giants were in only one area. They were the sons of Anak living in the city of Hebron, but fear made the ten spies think that giants were everywhere.)

Two spies, Joshua and Caleb, gave a report full of faith, and it was actually Caleb who said, "Let us go up at once and take possession, for we are well able to overcome it" (Num. 13:30; 14:6–9).

As you remember, the word of the ten prevailed, and the Lord said that as a result of the Israelites' fear and unbelief, they would have to wander forty extra years in the desert, until that generation of grumblers had died off and a new generation replaced them who would trust God and go into the land. The only exceptions who would actually get to enter: Joshua and Caleb.

Now Caleb, as a forty-year-old spy, had gotten his eye on the toughest part of the Promised Land—on Hebron, where the giants lived. And Moses, knowing his heart, promised him that someday, when the Israelites actually occupied the land, Hebron would be personally his. And that became Caleb's vision, the exciting view of his future from the Lord, which he knew would one day come true.

But then, what a B Zone Caleb went into! There was year after year of wandering around in the wilderness, while the Israelites continued to grumble, and eventually everybody his age was dying off. Caleb went into his fifties, sixties, seventies, eighties. . . .

Most of those around him were half his age. Was Caleb beginning to totter and forget things and reminisce too much? No way! He had stretched out his goals, and he knew his C Zone was ahead.

At last it was time to cross into the new land—and

who should be picked as leader but his colleague, the only other oldster, Joshua! No one hardly noticed old Caleb. Did that discourage him? Not at all. He stayed as physically and mentally fit as ever, waiting for his exciting future.

The Israelites defeated Jericho and many other towns and areas, and the land started to be parceled out among the tribes. Finally Caleb could wait no longer. He said to Joshua:

> I was forty years old when Moses . . . sent me . . . to explore the land. . . . So on that day Moses swore to me, "The land on which your feet have walked will be your inheritance and that of your children forever, because you have followed the LORD my God wholeheartedly."
>
> Now then, just as the LORD promised, he has kept me alive for forty-five years. . . . So here I am today, eighty-five years old! I am as strong today as the day Moses sent me out; I'm just as vigorous to go out to battle now as I was then. Now give me this hill country that the LORD promised me that day. You yourself heard then that the Anakites were there and their cities were large and fortified, but, the LORD helping me, I will drive them out just as he said (Josh. 14:7–12).

Joshua agreed, and the next thing we read is that Caleb had driven out three giants, sons of Anak, and settled his family in the place he'd so long been dreaming of (see Josh. 15:13–19).

To begin and persevere and win over a long haul, stretch out your goals and expectations, and pace yourself to achieve them.

Principle Two: *Choose creative work, and never quit.*

A. About choosing creative work. Did you ever notice that people in many kinds of occupations tend to burn out, but not artists? Symphony conductors, poets, and writers function into their eighties and nineties. Punching endless holes in metal on a factory assembly line seems to atrophy the mind; but creative work—maybe designing new shapes or uses for that metal—stimulates it.

When God said, "Let us make man in Our image," He did just that: He made us little creators, and we thrive when we are even feebly copying His business.

We heard someone say recently that every high school graduate should have been required to write a poem, play a musical instrument, or do something else creative! We dry up, we burn out, unless we're fresh to new ideas and open to new thoughts.

Keep the juices flowing! What new thing have you made, created, formed, all by yourself in the last six months? What new adventure have you had?

Stay in a position to grow. This means, always have some new A Zone in your life, something you're just learning to do, that you don't do well yet because it's new. That keeps you childlike, looking ahead to some new success.

The only thing you have to fear is fear!

Recently we were speaking in India and ran into an incredible couple, inspiring models for the two of us. They are Americans, Herb, age seventy-nine, and Helen, age seventy-four; they've been married two years. Since Herb's retirement as an Evangelical Covenant pastor, he's been four times to India, at his own expense, preaching every night in series of meetings here and there. They are both wiry and vigorous; they laugh a lot; they are obviously excited to be alive and to be useful and needed.

Only Helen was a little antsy: while on this trip in India, she was missing sessions of her class in computer programming!

Says a forum of Wheaton faculty members discussing the subject of creativity,

Creativity is not just about literature, music, drama, film, dance, statues or pictures. . . . Creativity is also about a wonderfully more elegant computer program, or a whole new approach to a scheduling system, or a perfect sermon illustration, or a way to remove grape juice stains from white cotton shirts. . . .

Creativity is also problem solving. . . .

High creativity chooses directions based on who God is and who man is and what is really important in life. High creativity moves toward freedom and healthy autonomy; low creativity moves toward conformity. High creativity puts technology to the service of human values; low technology makes people adapt to the system. . . .

The pressures of life seem perfectly calculated to harden our spirits and our minds into the safety of the known. The same prayer, the same sales pitch, the same system, the same joke, the same seat in church, the same friends, the same TV shows, the same solutions to the same problems. We are free and the door is open, but how often we stay in the cage! All we need to do is claim God's power to fulfill God's image in us, and we can thrill again to the continual renewing of our minds. All things can become new.[2]

In your place of work, there is something that needs improving. Can you get your mind going? Can you create, innovate, and suggest a plan? Melinda, our wonderful secretary-assistant for Renewal Ministries, did just that recently; she offered a great suggestion to solve a problem. It made us know how committed to our ministry Melinda is, and it gave the whole office a boost in morale!

If your mind is receptive and open, solutions to problems can come at any time. The composer Anton Bruckner (1824–1896) was asked once how he got his "divine" motif for his Ninth Symphony.

2. Dr. Richard Kriegbaum, "Creativity" (*In Form,* the Bulletin of Wheaton College, Oct. 1983), p. 1

"Well," he said, "I walked up the Kahlenberg, and when it got hot and I got hungry, I sat down by a little brook and unpacked my Swiss cheese. And just as I open the greasy paper, that darn tune pops in my head!"[3]

B. About never quitting. That doesn't mean not to retire. We heard someone say the other day that the Bible doesn't talk about retirement. Yes, it does: the priests of Levi were to do their work only from ages twenty-five to fifty! In our day that wouldn't seem a long enough work life.

But don't retire to unworthy purposes. One insurance company has reported that the average retiree receives only nineteen monthly retirement checks! For many, it would seem that when they quit working, they started to quit living.

Puttering isn't enough. You need something important and worthy to do, even if you don't need income and it's volunteer work. We see retirees all over the world who've started new careers as short-term missionaries and who are deeply appreciated and "having a ball."

Air Cal's flight magazine recently described "The Incredible World of Armand Hammer," chairman of the board and chief executive officer of Occidental Petroleum. The last paragraph of that article reads like this:

> "I have discovered the fountain of youth that keeps me young," says Dr. Hammer. "To keep accomplishing things. It is a form of creativeness. I get a great kick out of accomplishment, and it makes my adrenal glands function. I never feel my age, especially when I am about to make a deal. I mean, all my glands function better. I feel younger."

3. Quoted in Dr. Laurence J. Peter, *Peter's Quotations* (New York: Bantam Books, 1977), p. 123.

And Armand Hammer said all this at age 85![4]

Principle Three: *Forget yourself.*

When Welthy Fisher was in her nineties and on her way to speak at a conference, she slipped in a hallway and fell. She had a broken bone, and she couldn't move from off the floor until the doctor arrived.

With all her friends gathered around looking worried, she said, "Well, what are we waiting for? Pull up your chairs around me, and we'll go ahead with the conference."[5]

No wonder Welthy Fisher is now 103. She isn't full of herself, she's full of what she's doing and sharing!

Self-conscious, self-serving, self-gratifying, self-saving people don't wear well. They often don't survive a long time. They're the ones who inhabit the Q Zone.

To guard your relationships and your reputation over the years, to get loved rather than get obnoxious, you must choose to serve rather than to be served.

Serving is Jesus' way.

But over the years if you make more money, you begin to expect to be served. That's dangerous! We suppose one of the reasons "Ugly American" tourists get that title is because too often they expect to be waited on.

Never take service for granted. As long as you live, appreciate it; say thank you, encourage the server. And when you can, you be the one to wait on others.

We have a dear friend with a real estate company. It's not that his sixty employees are necessarily Christians, but every Christmas they go to convalescent homes. Our friend says, "It makes them happy to serve; it raises morale. And they need to do it."

4. *Air Cal,* March 1984, p. 51.
5. Jim Hefley, *Life Changes* (Wheaton, Ill.: Tyndale, 1984), p. 103.

There you are! Maintain a servant's heart. Let your question to others be, "What can I do to make you happy?" It's part of forgetting yourself. When your life is lived to help others, you'll probably stretch it out and make it better.

Herbert Lockyer wrote over sixty books. When he was just past ninety, he started on his 750,000-word *Nelson's Illustrated Bible Dictionary,* because he felt urgently that the Christian world needed it. He called it "the most colossal task of my life."

Dr. Lockyer lived in his own apartment in Colorado Springs. He researched and wrote six to seven hours a day, six days a week, and his life also included an exhausting speaking schedule. But God kept him very much alive through the age of ninety-eight to actually complete his Bible dictionary!

Forgetting yourself gives staying power!

We don't want to make it all sound too pat, too easy. Jim Hefler says, "To keep from getting old you'll have to fight stiff headwinds of social stereotypes, family expectations, and your own aches and pains."[6]

But keep choosing creative goals, stretching them out, forgetting yourself—and never quitting.

Stephen Jewett's classic study of New England oldsters produced these nine suggestions: Have—

1. A good heredity
2. Good marital and social relationships
3. Good physical health
4. Good work habits
5. Reduced anxiety
6. Optimism
7. Realism
8. Moderate eating habits, and

6. Ibid., p. 123.

9. A mind-set of faith.

Be glad if God gives you lots of years! After all, as Pablo Picasso said at eighty-six, "It takes a long time to become young."[7]

7. Quoted in "What Are You Going to Do with the Rest of Your Life?"—George Baxt. *Mainliner* magazine, March 1976, p. 27.

"You can't help
getting older,
but you don't
have to get
old"

—George Burns

CHAPTER 22

For Fun

Our family was recently looking at a picture in the paper of a man who weighs over eight hundred pounds.

Our son-in-law John remarked, "He didn't know when to quit."

We began making a list of things that should *not* have staying power. We'll show you our list; why don't you send us yours?

1. Banquets whose post dinner programs are bladder-busters;
2. The wedding kiss of a bride and groom;
3. A handshake when your ring is turned sideways;
4. A bath for your cat;
5. A boring person ("here today and here tomorrow");
6. A shower when there's no more hot water;
7. The ice-cream cone you're eating in August when you're wearing your very best clothes.

Then we thought of a few more things that *ought* to have staying power:

1. Your old car being test-driven around the block when you're trying to sell it;

2. The attentions of a boyfriend when you're thirty-eight and there's nobody else eligible around;
3. The ice-cream cone you're eating in January when you're wearing your old grubbies.

Any other contributions?

C H A P T E R 2 3

Begin, Persevere, Win!

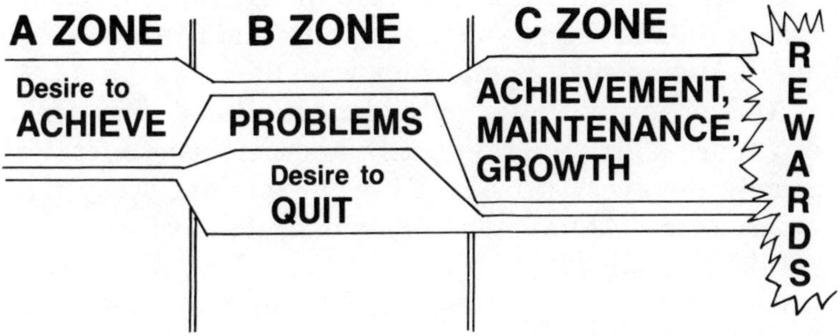

"Staying power."

Says the dictionary:

In sports, to "stay" means to successfully resist or hold off the opponent.

On a ship, a "stay" is a rope that resists winds and storms.

A corset has stays. Uh, you know what those stays are to hold back, or resist.

There are unwanted forces in your life, too, which you must hold off, hold back, resist. You know what they are.

And there's the time element: *How long* must you hold them off? Ask any member of Alcoholics Anonymous how long he has to resist liquor.

A team has to hold off the opponent until the game

ends. A ship's stay can't snap in the middle of a storm. And if a corset stay breaks halfway through dessert—well, *my dear.*

You've got to last all the way to the end. You've got to *begin and then persevere until you finally win!*

Friend, give life all you've got. Go for every C Zone you can find ahead of you, one at a time, no matter what the personal cost.

"I have resolved," said Jonathan Edwards, "that while I live, I shall live with all my might."

Go for the fullness of life! Live totally in God; tackle every problem before you, one by one; and live out every one of His marvelous plans for your life.

And when you think you've done it all and there isn't any more—give another push, another last spurt. Be greedy for every pressure, every exertion, every triumph, every achievement you can stretch for!

Like the ball player who went to his first horse race. Here came two horses madly pounding down the home stretch, one only inches ahead of the other. The crowd was going crazy. The finish line was getting closer and the excitement was reaching fever pitch. Amid all the shouting and the tumult, the ball player was roaring to the horse in front, "Slide, dummy, slide!"

That's the spirit.

. . . *Begin!*

Persevere!

Win!

But we don't want to end this book sounding at all flippant. The two of us are concerned that you, reader, and multitudes of others around the world, calm down and toughen up! Whatever your present situation, right now—

Look up to God, with strong faith; and

Look forward to your coming C Zone, with strong hope.

Then you will become "established, strengthened, settled." You'll have *staying power*—to last, and last well.

Let us know how you're doing.

Sincerely,

Dr. Raymond C. and Anne Ortlund
32 Whitewater Drive
Corona del Mar, CA 92625